DRAWING
THE LINES

DRAWING THE LINES

Constraints on Partisan
Gerrymandering in U.S. Politics

Nicholas R. Seabrook

CORNELL UNIVERSITY PRESS ITHACA AND LONDON

First published 2017 by Cornell University Press

Printed in the United States of America

Library of Congress Cataloging-in-Publication Data

Names: Seabrook, Nicholas R., author.
Title: Drawing the lines : constraints on partisan gerrymandering in U.S. politics / Nicholas R. Seabrook.
Description: Ithaca ; London : Cornell University Press, 2017. | Includes bibliographical references and index.
Identifiers: LCCN 2016030014 (print) | LCCN 2016031135 (ebook) | ISBN 9781501705311 (cloth : alk. paper) | ISBN 9781501707780 (Reflowable formats) | ISBN 9781501707797 (PDF ebook)
Subjects: LCSH: Gerrymandering—United States. | Apportionment (Election law)—United States.
Classification: LCC JK1341 .S39 2017 (print) | LCC JK1341 (ebook) | DDC 328.73/073455—dc23
LC record available at https://lccn.loc.gov/2016030014

Cornell University Press strives to use environmentally responsible suppliers and materials to the fullest extent possible in the publishing of its books. Such materials include vegetable-based, low-VOC inks and acid-free papers that are recycled, totally chlorine-free, or partly composed of nonwood fibers. For further information, visit our website at www.cornellpress.cornell.edu.

Contents

DRAWING
THE LINES

INTRODUCTION
Perceptions and Misperceptions of Partisan Redistricting

As the results of the 2002 election flashed across their television screens, Texas's congressional Republicans could be forgiven for feeling a certain amount of dissatisfaction with the redistricting process in the United States. Their party had seen its share of the statewide vote in U.S. House elections increase from 49.8 percent in 1992 to 54.9 percent in 2002. Yet, even with this latest ten-point victory over the Democrats in the popular vote, they had once again failed to convert their increasingly dominant electoral support into a Republican majority in the state's congressional delegation. A partisan gerrymander, passed in the wake of the 1990 Census and left largely intact by the district boundaries implemented by the federal courts following the 2000 Census, had allowed the Democratic Party to maintain its overall majority in the Texas delegation for more than a decade. The Democrats won twenty-one of Texas's thirty seats in Congress in 1992, and managed to retain control of nineteen in 1994 and seventeen from 1996 to 2000, despite averaging just 45.8 percent of the two-party vote in these elections. In 2003, the Texas Republicans, armed for the first time with control of both houses of the state legislature and the governorship, undertook an unprecedented mid-decade redrawing of the state's congressional boundaries. Though many Republicans in the state government were opposed to the idea of redrawing the district boundaries mid-decade, the effort was initiated under considerable pressure from Republicans in Congress, most notably House majority leader Tom DeLay (Kang 2005).

When Governor Rick Perry called a special session of the legislature to draw up the new map, fifty-nine Democrats in the Texas House, many of whom fled the state across the Oklahoma border in order to avoid arrest, boycotted the session to deprive the Republicans of a quorum. A second special session produced another Democratic exodus: this time, eleven Democratic senators fled to New Mexico. The Republicans responded by deploying state troopers to try to apprehend and return the missing Democrats, and attempting to enlist the help of the Justice Department and the Federal Aviation Administration in order to locate them, for which DeLay was later reprimanded by the House Ethics Committee (Hefley and Mollohan 2004).

Eventually, after one of the recalcitrant Democrats returned to Austin, Governor Perry called a third special session and the bill was finally passed. This unusual step of undertaking a mid-decade redistricting was termed a "perrymander," and the map itself was described by one journalist as resembling "an attempt to diagram an oil spill using Legos" (Ratliff 2003). Democrats decried the plan as an "outrageous partisan power grab" by "iron-fisted . . . far right-wing Republicans" (Ratcliffe, Hughes, and Raskin 2003). Republicans hailed it as a "historic advance in reorganizing government" that was "a real positive for the people of Texas" (Blumenthal 2003). In the 2004 election held under the newly redrawn district boundaries, the Republicans won 59.7 percent of the two-party congressional vote in Texas and took control of the state's delegation by a 21–11 margin.

The Texas example illustrates not only how contentious partisan control of the redistricting process has become but also how debates over redistricting reform have been framed by a basic assumption that partisan gerrymandering is fundamentally and self-evidently undemocratic and undesirable. In the wake of the subsequent court challenge, editorials appeared in major newspapers with headlines such as "Democracy's Bad Week" (*St. Louis Post Dispatch,* July 2, 2006), "The Court to Democracy: Drop Dead" (*Chicago Tribune,* July 2, 2006), and "Texas Massacre" (*Boston Globe,* June 29, 2006), while law review articles depicted the partisan gerrymander as "a pervasive and ever-expanding enterprise" (Katz 2007), and the Supreme Court's approach to redistricting litigation as "no longer empirically valid today" (Hirsch 2003). It is this level of conflict and controversy that has arisen in response to high-profile partisan gerrymanders and has seen the increasing involvement of the courts in redistricting litigation over the past several decades. The example of Texas is illustrative of a broader point: that the battle against partisan control of the redistricting process has been fierce, and it has been waged both in state legislatures and in the state and federal courts.

In reality, however, these efforts, though well-intentioned, are almost entirely misplaced. Effects attributed to partisan gerrymandering have been consistently demonstrated in the published political science literature to have mostly emanated not from deliberate manipulation of district boundaries, but instead from the natural impact of demographics and geography. As the Democratic Party has increasingly come to rely on urban and minority voters for its electoral coalition, their support has become more and more heavily concentrated in America's cities. Meanwhile, Republican voters tend to be considerably more evenly dispersed throughout the suburbs, exurbs, and in rural areas. As Democratic candidates run up huge margins of victory in many of the districts they represent, their Republican counterparts have tended to win their seats by far less lopsided majorities. Excluding uncontested seats, in U.S. House elections between 1992 and 2010, there were 427 races in which the Democratic candidate won more than 75 percent of the two-party vote, compared to just 108 for the Republicans. Forty-two Democrats managed to capture a staggering 90 percent or more of the popular vote even when facing a Republican opponent, while just two Republicans were able to achieve the same feat. The result is that even when districts are drawn at random by computers, significant partisan bias still emerges, and producing a hypothetical "unbiased" set of electoral boundaries often requires far more egregious manipulation of districts than any partisan gerrymander. The energy, activism, and litigation currently directed at ending the practice of partisan gerrymandering would be much better invested in ensuring basic fairness and competitiveness in U.S. House elections. Far more pernicious than a single party using redistricting to gain an electoral edge is the much more widespread phenomenon of incumbent politicians drawing uncompetitive districts to insulate themselves against the voters. The effect of this practice is to significantly undermine democratic accountability. Only by emphasizing competitiveness in districting can we ensure that the results of congressional elections are genuinely responsive to the will of the people.

Negative Perceptions of Partisan Redistricting

Partisan gerrymandering has been a controversial topic in American politics throughout the nation's entire political history. Critics of the practice—including many journalists (Chapman 2006; *Economist* 2002; Leavenworth 2010; Rosenbaum 2004), legal scholars (Dorf 2004; Greene 2005; Katz 2007; Lazarus 2003), and a number of political scientists (Grofman and King 2007; King et al. 2005)—have attacked partisan redistricting as a significant threat to democracy. It is alleged that the effects of redistricting are large and enduring enough to effectively dictate future election outcomes, thus subverting the will of the electorate and significantly undermining political competition. Nevertheless, despite several protracted litigation battles, the Supreme Court has consistently declined to rule the practice unconstitutional.

Besides the partisan electoral bias that gerrymandering can supposedly produce, opponents often highlight its suspected pernicious effects on electoral responsiveness. It has been blamed for declining levels of electoral competition, soaring incumbent reelection rates, and increased political polarization. Several states have responded to the perceived threat posed by partisan gerrymandering by taking redistricting powers away from the elected branches of government and vesting them in nonpartisan commissions that are supposed to redistrict using politically neutral criteria (to date, Arizona, California, Hawaii, Idaho, Iowa, Montana, New Jersey, and Washington have turned over control of congressional redistricting to independent or nonpartisan commissions). Between 1999 and 2006, proposals for creating redistricting commissions to prevent partisan gerrymandering of district boundaries were considered by state legislatures in an additional twenty-four states (Karch, McConnaughy, and Theriault 2007). In 2010, voters in Florida approved a ballot measure that amended the state's constitution to prohibit the legislature from redrawing legislative boundaries to favor any incumbent or political party (Jewett 2013). Allowing the political parties to control redistricting, it is alleged, has considerable negative consequences for democracy.

Many journalists also have gone on the attack against the gerrymander. An editorial in the *New York Times,* for instance, denounced partisan redistricting as a process for "making voters increasingly irrelevant," for "producing the least competitive Congressional elections in history" (March 1, 2006), and for creating a situation where "the House has become increasingly insulated from the voters because of gerrymandering that protects incumbents, reserves seats for particular parties and makes contested elections a rarity" (December 14, 2005). Similarly, the *Washington Post* lamented that gerrymandering "effectively foreclose[s] political participation . . . , and drive[s] ever-greater partisan polarization" (November 15, 2005), producing a situation where "the overwhelming majority of seats remain beyond serious democratic competition . . . , and incumbency still offer[s] surefire protection from voter dissatisfaction," and "House races are far from models of electoral accountability" (March 8, 2006).

Voters too seem to be dissatisfied with the current system, with a survey showing 67 percent of California likely voters expressing agreement with the statement that it is a "bad idea" for the legislature and governor to make decisions about redistricting (Public Policy Institute of California 2007). Another poll showed 66 percent in support of redistricting conducted by an independent commission, to just 21 percent in favor of redistricting by the state legislature (California Common Cause 2006). In a national poll, a plurality of 32 percent cited gerrymandering as the key reason for their dissatisfaction with the redistricting process, although it remains the case that many voters have little interest in or awareness of redistricting as an issue (Pew Research Center 2006). Fully 47 percent of registered voters did not know who was responsible for redrawing district boundaries, while 70 percent offered no opinion as to whether they were satisfied or dissatisfied with the way in which redistricting was conducted in their state.

A quick survey of law review articles on the topic of partisan gerrymandering reveals a similar hostility to the process within the legal community. Legal scholars generally reiterate many of the same claims about the subversion of democracy allegedly produced by partisan control of the redistricting process. With very few exceptions, articles appearing in major law reviews have approached the issue by attempting to come up with a constitutional standard by which the courts could declare the practice unconstitutional, and have criticized the Supreme Court for its unwillingness to take a stand against it. Legal commentators also decry partisan gerrymandering for its "contribution to the non-competitiveness of so many general election races" and "destructive polarization of our body politic" (Lazarus 2003). The judiciary is chastised for failing to strike a "blow against the corrupting influences of partisanship and incumbent self-preservation" (Lazarus 2003), an abrogation of their judicial duty in the face of "the threats to self-rule from non-competitive elections and sharp partisan division" that "consistently undermine the principles of democratic government" (Dorf 2004).

These journalistic and legal accounts are representative of a more generalized hostility to partisan conflict (Hibbing and Theiss-Morse 1995, 2002; Hofstadter 1970; Ranney 1975) and a deeper skepticism toward parties as institutions. More than a third of Americans now identify themselves as political independents, though their behavior reveals the majority of them to be closet partisans (Keith et al. 1992). Furthermore, significant parallels to the modern redistricting reform movement can be seen more than a century ago in the efforts during the Progressive Era to undercut the power of the party machines, where reforms such as the ballot initiative and the direct primary also sought to transfer political power away from the arena of party politics. This evidence is indicative of a conventional wisdom that exists in the United States that partisan control of the redistricting process is a fundamental and pervasive threat to democracy, part of a broader unease that Americans have always had with the perceived machinations of the party system.

Contemporary policy debates are too often either ill-informed or ignorant of the actual systematic effects that redistricting has on election outcomes. Accounts often focus instead on anecdotal or short-term evidence, while ignoring the long-term implications that control of the redistricting process can have for democracy, both positive and negative. It is also evident that, in many instances, policy positions on redistricting are driven by ideology and partisan self-interest rather than by a careful consideration of the evidence. The positions of the Democratic and Republican Parties on two 2005 ballot initiatives, one in Ohio and the other in California, provide an ideal illustration of this. In Ohio, the Democratic-supported initiative to create an independent redistricting commission was defeated 70–30 due to the opposition of Republicans and Republican-affiliated interest groups. In the same year in California, a similar proposal, this time backed by state Republicans and opposed by Democrats and Democratic-affiliated interest groups, was also defeated by a 60–40 majority. The pattern is clear: in both states, the majority party—Democrats in California, Republicans in Ohio—was opposed to giving up its own control over the redistricting process, while in the other state, members of the same party, now in the minority, suddenly became proponents of good government reform. Opinion on redistricting, therefore, at both the elite and mass levels, is often influenced by partisan and ideological interests and by distrust of political parties as institutions.

Partisan Gerrymandering and the Law

The U.S. Constitution itself has little to say on the subject of redistricting, providing only in Article I, Section 2 for the apportionment of congressional seats between the states on the basis of population, and in Article I, Section 4 for members of the House of Representatives to be selected "by the people." In practice, states themselves have determined the logistics of House elections, dividing their congressional seats among districts in which voters can directly elect their own representatives. While the Constitution does give Congress the power to "make or alter" the electoral regulations for congressional elections (Article I, Section 4), Congress has to date been content to leave redistricting largely in the hands of the states. Currently, the only requirement that states must follow under federal statutory law when conducting redistricting is that their congressional delegation be elected from single-member districts. This has not always been the case. As the late U.S. Supreme Court justice Antonin Scalia has pointed out, an examination of the historical record reveals that, "the power bestowed on Congress to regulate elections, and in particular to restrain the practice of political gerrymandering, has not lain dormant" (541 U.S. 276). At various times, Congress has imposed both contiguity and compactness requirements on the states, as well as a mandate that House districts contain approximately equal populations. Though these restrictions were renewed in apportionment legislation passed by Congress in 1911, they have not thereafter been required, and only the single-member district mandate still remains. With some exceptions, then, the vast majority of states have throughout their history vested the power to determine the boundaries of congressional and state legislative districts in their own legislatures, thus allowing politicians to control the fundamental rules of the electoral game, and perhaps to use that control to bolster their own electoral fortunes, as well as those of their partisan allies.

Justice Scalia further noted in his discussion of redistricting that "political gerrymanders are not new to the American scene" (541 U.S. 274). In fact, examples of the manipulation of electoral boundaries in the interests of altering the distribution of political representation can be found even before the American Revolution, such as the early eighteenth-century attempt by the colony of Pennsylvania to blunt the political power of the city of Philadelphia by refusing to allow it to consolidate with surrounding jurisdictions, or the 1732 attempt by the governor of the province of North Carolina to divide and alter the boundaries of assembly precincts to benefit his political allies (Griffith 1974). It is also clear that the issue of gerrymandering, though not yet known by that name, was on the minds of many of the framers during debates over the drafting and ratification of the Constitution. The "make or alter" clause was included in the Constitution, according to James Madison, in order to provide a check against potential partisan manipulation of the electoral process at the state level, while Madison himself was allegedly the victim of an unsuccessful attempt by Patrick Henry to gerrymander him out of the 1st Congress (Rives 1970).

By far the most famous historical example, however, and the one from which the practice derives its name, was the 1812 attempt by the eponymous Elbridge Gerry to redraw the state legislative boundaries in Massachusetts to benefit the Democratic-Republicans over the Federalists. Gerry's plan included the infamous "salamander" district that has become the symbol of the gerrymander in books, articles, and political cartoons ever since. It must be noted that Gerry's name was actually pronounced with a hard *g*, as in gecko; however, the portmanteau "gerrymander," first coined by the *Boston Gazette* in 1812, over time has come to be pronounced with a soft *g*, so as to mimic the name of the mischievous MGM cartoon mouse. This particular pronunciation battle, I fear, is one that has been lost to the ages. Griffith (1974, 123) argues that "by 1840 the gerrymander was a recognized force in party politics and was generally attempted in all legislation enacted for the formation of election districts. It was generally conceded that each party would attempt to gain power which was not proportionate to its numerical strength." This trend toward greater use of the redistricting as a tool for the pursuit of partisan and political goals has only been exacerbated following the Supreme Court's involvement in the "reapportionment revolution" of the mid-twentieth century. Since the court's decision in *Wesberry v. Sanders* (376 U.S. 1 (1964)), which required that all congressional districts within a state be of approximately equal population, gerrymandering has emerged as the key method by which politicians have been able to use their control over districting in order to attempt to exert influence on the electoral process. At the same time, the redistricting cycles of the 1970s, 1980s, 1990s, and 2000s have seen both a significant growth in political controversy surrounding gerrymandering, and the rise of litigation filed at both the federal and state levels as a vehicle for taking on the practice.

High-profile and controversial redistricting, such as the one that occurred in Texas in 2003, is not the norm. However, it has become emblematic of the problems that many see in how redistricting has been performed by the political branches of state government. Anecdotes of this sort have fueled redistricting reform, and views have been reinforced by the Supreme Court's involvement in several high-profile recent partisan gerrymandering cases, including one that stemmed directly from the 2003 Texas plan. Following the Supreme Court's initial foray into partisan gerrymandering disputes in the case of *Davis v. Bandemer* (478 U.S. 109 (1986)), the issue largely disappeared from the court's docket for almost two decades. *Bandemer*'s precedent, which has since been interpreted and applied by lower federal courts as the law of the land, established a judicial test for identifying what constitutes unconstitutional partisan gerrymandering. This standard—which required that a challenged gerrymander be demonstrated not simply to put a party at an electoral disadvantage, but to be so effective and long-lasting as to shut them out of the political process entirely—is so high that just a single redistricting plan has been struck down by the courts under the test since its establishment. This one exception was the case of *Republican Party of North Carolina v. Martin* (1992), which struck down North Carolina's statewide system of electing superior court judges, a system that had resulted in the election of only one Republican judge since 1900. Not only did this case arguably misapply the *Bandemer* precedent since it did not involve the drawing of district lines, but just five days after the district court announced its decision, and concluded that the statewide method of electing judges "had resulted in Republican candidates experiencing a consistent and pervasive lack of success and exclusion from the electoral process as a whole and that these effects were likely to continue unabated into the future," the Republican Party won every contested seat in the elections for superior court judgeships (Kang 2005). On appeal, and finding this result to be "directly at odds with the recent prediction by the district court," the Fourth Circuit Court of Appeals overruled the decision in *Republican Party of North Carolina v. Hunt* (1996).

Taking up the issue again in *Vieth v. Jubelirer* (541 U.S. 267 (2004)) and *League of United Latin American Citizens v. Perry* (548 U.S. 399 (2006)), the Supreme Court essentially retained the central holding of the *Bandemer* precedent, concluding there is no evidence that partisan gerrymandering has sufficiently damaging or long-lasting effects on the minority party's voters to constitute an Equal Protection Clause violation. While opposition to partisan gerrymandering has been widespread, little progress has been made in the courtroom toward curtailing the practice.

Going Beyond the Conventional Wisdom

Two central assumptions underlie the negative reaction that many seem to have to the prospect of political parties controlling the redrawing of congressional and state legislative boundaries. The first is that partisan control of the redistricting process has widespread and significant electoral effects, a claim that is repeated in many of the editorials and law review articles urging the courts to step in and strike down the practice. The second is that the effects of partisan redistricting are exclusively negative—gerrymandering leads to partisan bias and reduced competition, and is therefore inherently an impediment to the proper operation of democracy. The purpose of this book is to empirically evaluate the validity of each of these assumptions and, in so doing, to question the conventional wisdom about congressional redistricting in the United States.

Chapter 1 outlines the central theoretical argument: that congressional redistricting, whether by a single party or by other means, is a fundamentally constrained activity, and that the nature of these constraints have significant implications for both bias and responsiveness. The result is that the effects of redistricting are conditional—partisan bias is created only under a limited set of circumstances, and any bias injected into the electoral system by redistricting will tend to erode over subsequent electoral cycles. The reason for this is the high degree of uncertainty that exists about future election outcomes. Not only can population migration significantly alter the configuration of a district over subsequent election cycles, but changing turnout patterns, generational replacement, and the impact of national electoral swings can also fundamentally alter the composition of the electorate on which a gerrymander was based.

Furthermore, the nature of redistricting creates a situation where a focus on partisan goals has different implications for competitiveness, depending on who is in control of the process. Where one political party has unified control of state government, the partisan goal becomes the creation of an efficient political gerrymander, which has positive implications for electoral competition. At the same time, the displacement of district populations also increases competitiveness by severing the link between incumbents and their constituents, thus undermining the incumbency advantage. Where control of state government is divided, both parties are veto players in the redistricting process. The partisan goal now becomes to secure a compromise that protects the party's existing electoral strength, with both parties having incentives to implement a redistricting plan that reduces electoral competition and insulates their incumbents against the will of the public.

Chapters 2 and 3 delve more deeply into the legal debates over partisan gerrymandering. I undertake a critical analysis of the involvement of the U.S. Supreme Court in litigation relating to partisan gerrymandering, paying particular attention to how the central arguments contained in the Supreme Court's precedent, as applied by the lower federal courts, are supported or refuted by empirical realities. Chapter 2 focuses on the first of two major Supreme Court cases that dealt with the issue of political gerrymandering and attempted to apply the previously established *Bandemer* precedent to congressional elections: the 2004 case of *Vieth v. Jubelirer*; whereas chapter 3 concentrates on the court's most recent foray into this issue: the 2006 case of *League of United Latin American Citizens v. Perry*. While a great deal has been written on these decisions, accounts have generally focused on whether the court set too high a standard for finding a gerrymander unconstitutional, resulting in just a single instance being overturned by the lower federal courts. I argue that the standard was neither excessively high nor inconsistent, but that the federal courts have failed to overturn a gerrymander because their effects are generally not that long-lasting. This conclusion is bolstered through case studies of the states involved in these cases: Pennsylvania and Texas. Detailed analysis of the subsequent election results reveals that the court's cautious approach appears to have been vindicated, as there is little to no evidence of long-term electoral disadvantage being created for the party that was targeted by each of the challenged partisan gerrymanders.

In chapters 4 and 5, I conduct two major empirical analyses that test a number of hypotheses derived from the theoretical argument in chapter 1 and the legal evidence in chapters 2 and 3. Chapter 4 analyzes the extent to which partisan redistricting creates long-term partisan distortions in congressional elections compared to other types of redistricting, and investigates the magnitude of these effects. I compare different redistricting methods in terms of their impact on two measures of partisan bias, or the extent to which an electoral system, as compared to some neutral standard, favors one of the two major political parties over the other. The results suggest that partisan gerrymandering can produce a small but sometimes persistent bias in favor of the party that implemented the redistricting plan.

Chapter 5 analyzes the effects of partisan gerrymandering on electoral responsiveness and district-level competitiveness when compared to bipartisan redistricting. I also examine the unintended consequences that the recent emphasis in the redistricting reform movement on advocating the use of independent or bipartisan commissions may have for subsequent congressional elections. The results suggest that, rather than reacting to the perceived negative consequences of partisan gerrymandering, which are found to have little or no empirical basis, redistricting reforms should instead be focused on reducing the deleterious effects that bipartisan redistricting has on electoral competition.

Finally, I conclude by summarizing the findings of the previous empirical, textual, and case study analyses, and discussing the implications that the results have for future redistricting reform efforts.

Considered as a whole, this book brings a new approach to the study of redistricting, blending political science and legal studies research in an investigation of the effects of partisan gerrymandering on U.S. House elections. I first use close analysis of the Supreme Court's partisan gerrymandering jurisprudence to frame hypotheses about the effects of redistricting on congressional elections, which I then subject to rigorous empirical testing using data on all U.S. House elections from 1990 to 2010, spanning two full redistricting cycles. The results suggest that partisan gerrymandering poses far less of a threat to democratic accountability than the conventional wisdom would indicate.

I also contend that the Supreme Court has been correct to take a cautious approach to cases challenging the constitutionality of the practice of partisan gerrymandering since the potential effects of gerrymandering are often mitigated by the significant constraints on the redistricting process and, where present, manifest themselves largely in the short term. Furthermore, partisan gerrymandering has no detrimental effects on district-level electoral competition and, in fact, leads to higher levels of competitiveness than the most frequently used alternative of bipartisan redistricting. I conclude the book with suggestions about how these empirical findings may guide future redistricting reform efforts and litigation that will undoubtedly follow during subsequent redistricting cycles, as well as how the redistricting process might be used to increase the competitiveness of congressional elections.

This is by no means an exhaustive treatment of redistricting in the United States. Though much has been written before on the topic of partisan gerrymandering, and much will undoubtedly be written subsequent to this analysis, this book undertakes the first comprehensive examination of the legal and political implications of partisan and bipartisan control of the redistricting process in the two most recent congressional redistricting cycles. In so doing, the analysis goes beyond simply asking *who* redraws the House, as so many accounts of redistricting in the United States are wont to focus on, and endeavors to systematically uncover the effects that current redistricting practices have on the proper functioning of a representative democracy. An informed debate on the future of redistricting policy in the United States demands nothing less.

A THEORY OF CONSTRAINED REDISTRICTING

The central theoretical foundation of my argument and the subsequent analysis is that congressional redistricting operates under a significant number of constraints. Those responsible for redrawing electoral boundaries must accede to an array of constitutional, institutional, statutory, geographic, and political demands that limit their ability to pursue partisan goals. Because of these constraints, it is very difficult to implement a redistricting plan that institutes severe and long-lasting electoral bias. The nature of the efficient gerrymander, whereby voters of the opposing party are packed into a few safe districts with large majorities of wasted votes, while others are cracked into more competitive adjacent districts that the gerrymandering party hopes to capture by smaller margins, renders it inherently unstable and susceptible to adverse national trends in subsequent elections.

The reason for this is that gerrymandering can only produce distorted electoral outcomes if one party's support is more efficiently distributed across the electoral landscape than the other's. As safe seats only serve to reduce overall vote efficiency by creating large numbers of wasted votes, a highly efficient vote distribution necessarily requires a party to win seats by smaller majorities. The more dramatically districts are redrawn in order to benefit a particular party, the greater the erosion of the strong incumbency advantage that exists in congressional elections. The implication of this is that a focus in the redistricting process on partisan goals, rather than incumbency, should have a net positive effect on the competitiveness of U.S. House elections.

These constraints on the redistricting process fall into one of several categories: political constraints, which concern the nature of the redistricting process as it is conducted in the United States and the inherent uncertainty about its effects; legal constraints, which concern the various constitutional and statutory provisions that redistricters must follow when redrawing the district boundaries; structural constraints, which concern the historical and institutional frameworks that redistricting must operate within; and geographic constraints, which concern the underlying populations and voter alignments that redistricting seeks to allocate among the various districts in a given political jurisdiction.

Political Constraints on Redistricting

As with all decisions made by the political branches of government, redistricting must operate within the rules and procedures of the existing democratic process. In the vast majority of U.S. states, the redrawing of congressional district boundaries after each decennial census is the responsibility of the people's representatives in their state government.

Control of State Government

With limited exceptions, a necessary condition for the implementation of a partisan gerrymander is for one political party to control each of the political branches of state government (both legislative chambers and the governorship) at the time of reapportionment following the decennial census. There are two situations where this may not be the case. First, most states also allow a gubernatorial veto of a redistricting plan to be overridden by a two-thirds majority in both legislative chambers, and so a party with a supermajority in both houses of the state legislature may implement a partisan redistricting scheme even without controlling the governorship. This occurred in 2002, both in Massachusetts, where a Democratic plan was passed over the veto of Republican governor Swift, and in Arkansas, where a Democratic plan was passed without the signature of Republican governor Huckabee, who lacked the votes to sustain a veto (Congressional Quarterly 2008). Second, several states have laws that limit the role of the governor in the redistricting process, thus allowing a party that controls the legislature but lacks a supermajority the opportunity to implement a gerrymander. These are Tennessee, which allows a gubernatorial veto of a redistricting plan to be overridden by a simple majority in both houses, and Connecticut and North Carolina, which do not allow a gubernatorial veto of a congressional redistricting plan. Several other states allow vetoes of congressional plans, but not those for the state house or state senate (Voting and Democracy Research Center 2004). For the two most recent redistricting cycles, partisan control of the redistricting process was dictated by the results of the 1990 and 2000 state legislative elections, and the corresponding gubernatorial elections for terms expiring no earlier than 1991 and 2001.

There are currently eight states that conduct congressional redistricting using an independent nonpartisan commission, most recently California, which established a Citizens Redistricting Commission following the voters' approval of Proposition 11 in 2008. In addition, six states, consisting of Connecticut, Illinois, Indiana, Mississippi, Oklahoma, and Texas, have constitutional or statutory provisions that require redistricting to be referred to an independent commission if the legislature fails to pass a reapportionment plan by a certain deadline (National Conference of State Legislatures 2008). In the 2000 redistricting cycle, such provisions were triggered by deadlocked legislatures in Connecticut and Indiana (Karch, McConnaughy, and Theriault 2007). Partisan manipulation of the congressional district boundaries in the remaining forty-two states, except in the case of the exceptions noted above, requires unified partisan control of each of the branches of state government. Redistricting plans must be passed by both houses of the state legislature and signed into law by the governor, allowing a minority party in control of just one of these branches to thwart the majority's wishes and force them to compromise on redistricting. Even with unified state government, a combination of institutional rules, delaying tactics, and legislative logrolling may allow a minority party to exert some influence over the redistricting process, perhaps limiting the ability of the majority to implement an effective unilateral partisan gerrymander. This might not be a significant obstacle if unified state government were the norm in the United States; however, this has not been the case in recent decades.

In the wake of the 2000 election, when the vast majority of congressional redistricting schemes were being drawn up, just twenty-three states had unified partisan control of all three branches of state government. In only thirteen of these, however, was there the potential for partisan gerrymandering of congressional districts. North Dakota, South Dakota, Montana, and Wyoming each had unified partisan state government, but only a single at-large congressional district. Arizona, Hawaii, Idaho, New Jersey, and Washington also had unified state government, but conducted redistricting through independent commissions. Congressional districts in Mississippi, which had unified Democratic control, were redrawn by the courts. Nebraska was the only state with a unicameral nonpartisan legislature, and so cannot be included in the total of states with unified partisan control. For the purposes of this analysis, redistricting in Nebraska was coded as bipartisan. Vermont, in addition to being a state with an at-large congressional district, and Maine had independent governors at the time of redistricting, and so are also coded as bipartisan. In the 1990s, just twenty states had unified partisan control, and in only sixteen of these was there the potential for partisan gerrymandering. The states excluded were South Dakota, an at-large state; Hawaii, which uses an independent redistricting commission; and Florida and Mississippi, whose congressional districts were redrawn by the courts.

The norm in the most recent redistricting cycles has been divided state government, which requires the parties to compromise on the redrawing of electoral boundaries. Partisan gerrymandering is generally not a widespread phenomenon in the United States, and may become even less frequent as state elections become more competitive and divided state government becomes more frequent (Jewell and Morehouse 2001), although the results of the 2010 and 2012 elections indicate that this pattern may be reversing itself.

In states without partisan control of state government in the legislative session immediately following the decennial census, redistricting must involve some degree of compromise between competing political interests. Political parties in some states have attempted to circumvent this constraint by conducting so-called mid-decade redistricting, whereby a party that takes control of state government in an election subsequent to redistricting uses this opportunity to conduct partisan redistricting through an additional redrawing of the electoral boundaries. Though the possibility has been discussed by politicians in a number of states in recent years (Cook 2005), mid-decade partisan redistricting has occurred on only two occasions since the 2000 census: first, in 2003, where it was instigated by Republicans in Texas after they gained control of the state House of Representatives; and again in 2005, at the behest of Republicans in Georgia after they were able to capture control of the governorship and state legislature. A similar effort was undertaken by Republicans in Colorado after they took control of the state senate in 2002, but it was struck down by the Colorado Supreme Court as a violation of Colorado's state constitution (*Salazar v. Davidson*, 79 P.3d 1221 (Colo. 2003)).

Incumbency

Gelman and King (1994, 541–42) and Campbell (1996, 126–27) both argue that the redrawing of electoral boundaries is also constrained by the fundamental tension between the competing interests of partisan advantage and incumbent protection. As participants in redistricting, incumbent state legislators have an interest in their own future electoral fortunes, as well as those of their party. Incumbent members of Congress, although not directly responsible for redrawing their own district boundaries, are nonetheless involved in the redistricting process through lobbying or other informal influence. For example, Republican House majority leader Tom DeLay was an instrumental player in Texas's 2003 redistricting, the purpose of which was by his own admission to increase Republican representation in the House of Representatives. Any redistricting effort, whether partisan or bipartisan, must at least be cognizant of, and in some cases may even be dictated by, the need for incumbent protection arising from mutual self-interest. In bipartisan redistricting, where control of state government is split between the major political parties, there is little potential for either party to gain an electoral advantage through gerrymandering. Bipartisan redistricting therefore allows incumbents greater influence over the drawing of district boundaries, as both parties have incentives to compromise in order to preserve their existing electoral strength. With both parties as veto players in the redistricting process, failure to cooperate most likely leads to redistricting by the judiciary or another independent body, with unpredictable results that both sides have incentive to avoid. Such redistricting tends to result in compromises that benefit incumbents of both parties, protecting their seats and preserving to a significant degree the existing electoral alignment. A good example of this is the state of New York, where divided partisan control of the two houses of the state legislature has been the norm for the last several redistricting cycles, with the Republican Party controlling the state senate from 1965 to 2009, and the Democratic Party having been in the majority in the state assembly since 1975. Successive redistricting has served to preserve and often reinforce this alignment, which was not broken until the Democrats gained a narrow majority in the state senate following the 2008 election (one they quickly lost again in 2010).

When one party controls the redistricting process and intends to implement a partisan gerrymander, the interests of incumbent protection and partisan advantage are in direct competition with one other. A party may gerrymander conservatively and focus on packing its opponents into safe districts while simultaneously protecting its own incumbent candidates, but the efficient gerrymander necessarily involves the creation of competitive seats that the gerrymandering party's incumbents must defend (Friedman and Holden 2008). The primary interest of partisan redistricting is to target incumbents of the opposing party, either by redrawing them into districts where they must face off against another incumbent, a practice known as pairing, or by redrawing them into marginal districts that the gerrymandering party hopes to capture. It is therefore likely that the net effect of partisan gerrymandering, as compared to bipartisan collusion, will be to create increased incumbent vulnerability, competitiveness, and turnover of legislative seats.

Any attempt to manipulate the House electoral boundaries to the advantage of one party over the other also necessarily involves a party giving up votes in some districts in order to increase its overall number of legislative seats. Even allowing for retirements and changes in apportionment, some incumbent representatives of the party in control of redistricting may have to sacrifice a portion of their own electoral strength and safety in order to further the collective interests of the party. When a party in control of redistricting seeks to target an opposing incumbent by removing blocs of supporters from his or her district, geographic constraints may dictate that those voters be redrawn into the districts of incumbents of the gerrymandering party, therefore diluting those incumbents' electoral strength. The high degree of uncertainty about future outcomes thus provides incentives for redistricters to be conservative when redrawing the electoral boundaries, in order to protect the electoral interests of incumbent candidates, and the effectiveness of partisan gerrymandering is constrained by this tension between the competing goals of incumbent protection and partisan advantage. Where redistricting does pursue partisan goals, as opposed to incumbent protection, the expectation is that this will have a positive effect on overall electoral competition.

Self-Constraints, Uncertainty, and Risk Aversion

Analyses of the effects of partisan redistricting generally pay little attention to the actual practicalities of the redistricting process itself, and the logistics of redrawing district boundaries in such a way as to benefit one political party over another. Partisan gerrymandering is generally accomplished by two principal strategies that act in tandem with one other to maximize the effective votes of one party while minimizing those of another. The first of these strategies is "cracking," which refers to the practice of breaking up the targeted party's geographical bases of support into several different districts, thus diluting their votes and reducing their efficiency. These supporters are thereby unable to vote in sufficient concentrations to win the individual seats into which they are divided, even though they may represent a significant enough voting bloc overall to warrant representation (Butler and Cain 1992).

The second strategy is "packing," which refers to the practice of combining the targeted party's geographical bases of support into a few supermajority districts, thus wasting significant numbers of their votes in a small number of overwhelming victories and allowing the party in control of redistricting to capture neighboring seats. Partisan gerrymandering is generally accomplished using a combination of these tactics to pack some of the targeted party's voters into districts where they constitute a large majority, while cracking the rest of their voters into districts where they are only slightly in the minority. The intended effect is for the targeted party to win a few districts by large majorities with many wasted votes, whereas the gerrymandering party wins a large number of districts by small majorities and a highly efficient vote distribution (Cox and Katz 2002).

The inherent dangers in this practice are immediately evident: the greater reward a party seeks to gain from partisan gerrymandering, the greater risk it must take in implementing it. The capacity for a gerrymander to distort election results depends on the ability of the party that controls redistricting to capture seats by marginal majorities and hold on to them in subsequent elections. With each additional election conducted under a set of gerrymandered boundaries, it becomes increasingly difficult to predict the behavior of voters, the migration patterns of registered partisans, and the entry of new voters into the electorate. The result is that the marginal districts a party was able to capture through redistricting may be lost as a result of relatively small national swings in the popular vote and coattail effects. Artificial majorities created by gerrymanders are often unstable and may be prone to swing back toward parity in subsequent electoral cycles, suggesting that while gerrymandering may be an effective tool for a party to increase its electoral representation in the short term, in the long term, its effects are uncertain.

The strategy of cracking and packing in an attempt to maximize overall vote efficiency in search of the "efficient gerrymander" is thus a dangerous strategy for redistricters to pursue due to the uncertainty about long-term effects. When a future election produces even a relatively minor popular vote swing against the party implementing a gerrymander, the seats they are able to capture by maximizing vote efficiency are extremely susceptible to reverting back to the opposition party's control. For this very reason, some recent research has cast doubt on the utility of the efficient gerrymander as accomplished through a combination of cracking and packing. It suggests that focusing exclusively on packing, while yielding smaller short-term gains for the party controlling redistricting, may produce longer-lasting and more durable partisan effects in the presence of uncertainty about voter preferences (Friedman and Holden 2008).

The strategy they choose to pursue, therefore, has significant implications for a party that controls redistricting in a state. When redistricters focus on increasing short-term partisan gains rather than promoting long-term stability, they are arguably behaving suboptimally. The practice of partisan gerrymandering, with its focus on capturing a large number of seats by small margins in order to maximize overall vote efficiency, should produce an increase in the competitiveness of electoral districts, thus making the gerrymander inherently unstable. When a party pursues the optimal gerrymandering strategy, focusing on increasing vote efficiency by packing its opponents and reducing wasted votes in the districts it loses, rather than creating marginal seats to reduce wasted votes in the districts it wins, it is necessarily limiting its short-term partisan gains. Given the high level of uncertainty, risk aversion may act as a self-constraint on legislators when implementing a partisan gerrymander, thereby reducing their ability to significantly distort subsequent elections results.

Displacement of District Populations

Not only are redistricters often risk-averse in the face of significant uncertainty about the effects of redistricting, preferring to create safe districts rather than the marginal seats that might help the party capture the maximum number of seats in an advantageous electoral climate, but even parties in complete control of redistricting within a particular state often do not take the opportunity to gerrymander extensively, preferring instead to preserve the cores of existing districts as much as possible. For example, Democrats controlled both the legislature and the governorship in California following the 2000 election, and saw the state gain an extra seat in the House of Representatives as a result of the 2000 census. However, the party elected not to make extensive changes to the existing district alignment, choosing not to make use of its unilateral control of the redistricting process to gerrymander the state's congressional districts in its favor.

Why might a party decline the opportunity to remake the electoral map to its advantage? The explanation may be found in the literature on the incumbency advantage in U.S. House elections, and in particular in the concept of the personal vote (Ansolabehere, Snyder, and Stewart 2000). This component of the incumbency advantage, which goes along with other factors such as candidate quality and the voting cues that incumbency and name recognition provide for low-information voters, encapsulates the goodwill that incumbents are able to build up over time through responsiveness to their constituents and the funding they secure for their districts, or what Richard Fenno (1978) termed their "home style." The personal vote makes up a large fraction of the incumbency advantage, somewhere in the region of 50–70 percent, and has been shown to be larger in areas where incumbents are electorally most vulnerable (Ansolabehere, Snyder, and Stewart 2000).

When redistricting occurs, however, and large numbers of voters are transferred into new districts where their link with their previous incumbent House member is severed, the personal vote component of the incumbency advantage is significantly undermined. While the personal vote costs of redistricting—the implications of incumbents facing significant numbers of new voters in the next election—had been previously thought to be relatively small and predictable, more recent research has demonstrated that incumbents face significant costs from being forced to run for reelection in districts with large numbers of new voters, even if the partisan alignment of their district has not changed all that significantly. Using a new measure of the incumbency advantage, which sees it as a function of short-term effects, partisanship, and electoral saliency, Desposato and Petrocik (2003) demonstrate that new voters are more susceptible to short-term political forces, and weak partisans are more likely to fall back into partisan voting following redistricting. This effect persists beyond first election, but is reduced as incumbents start to build up their personal vote again in subsequent elections. The upshot is that incumbents face very real electoral consequences when redistricting redraws new voters into their districts, and these effects are greatest when major changes are made to existing district populations.

McKee (2008) demonstrates that this effect significantly hurt Democratic incumbents in the elections of 1992 and 1994. Despite controlling redistricting in a number of southern states, Democrats were unable to use their control to insulate their existing electoral strength against the subsequent Republican tide. One major reason for this was that the electoral maps in these states needed to be retooled extensively to abide by the legal requirements of "one person, one vote" and the creation of majority-minority districts. The result was that new voters drawn into districts represented by Democratic incumbents, lacking the personal vote connection, were more likely to vote Republican in subsequent elections due to short-term factors like candidate quality, fund-raising, and the political climate (Petrocik and Desposato 1998). The one exception to this pattern was Texas, where Democrats benefited from the additional flexibility of three newly created districts that the state gained as a result of the 1990 census (Black and Black 2002). In another study, Yoshinaka and Murphy (2011) argue that redistricters can use this knowledge strategically to foster more instability for opposing incumbents in enacting partisan gerrymanders, thus reducing the electoral strength of opposing partisans without affecting the partisan balance of their districts. Bipartisan redistricting, they argue, leads to the lowest level of instability as it protects the districts of incumbents of both parties, while neutral plans should produce the highest instability since they do not take incumbency into account at all. The problems created by displacement of district populations are another constraint that redistricters face when attempting to use the process for partisan advantage.

Legal Constraints on Redistricting

In many states, those tasked with conducting redistricting for either the state legislature or the U.S. House of Representatives are not free to impose any set of district boundaries they please. Though in theory it might be possible to make use of sophisticated Geographic Information Systems (GIS) and data on partisan voting trends to configure the districts in such a way as to create an efficient partisan gerrymander, in reality, there are certain constraints imposed by federal and state statutory and constitutional law that limit the degree to which district boundaries can be manipulated during redistricting.

State Constitutional and Statutory Requirements

One way in which redistricters face legal constraints in the redrawing of boundaries is through the inclusion of compactness requirements in many state constitutions. These relate to the overall shape of the districts in a given electoral map. Compactness is defined as the distance from each point along a district's boundary to the centroid of that district, with the most compact district therefore being one where every point along the circumference is equidistant from the central point (a circular district). Compactness requirements impose a degree of regularity on the configuration of district boundaries, thus precluding the drawing of large numbers of irregularly shaped districts in the pursuit of partisan goals. There is no universally agreed on definition or standard for gauging or measuring the compactness of legislative districts. Political scientists have developed more than two dozen indices for gauging district compactness, but the approach taken to identifying malcompactness in challenged redistricting plans has been more akin to Justice Stewart's famous definition of obscenity in *Jacobellis v. Ohio* (1964)—"I know it when I see it" (Monmonier 2001, 64–65). As table 1.1 illustrates, seventeen states currently have some form of compactness requirement written into their redistricting laws (Voting and Democracy Research Center

TABLE 1.1.   Legal Constraints on Redistricting by State

Compactness Requirements (17 States):

AL, AZ, IA, ID, KS, KY, MD, MN, MO, MS, NE, NH, NV, SC, UT, WA, WV
Contiguity Requirements (19 States):

AL, AZ, CA, GA, IA, ID, KS, MD, MN, MO, MS, NC, NE, NH, OR, SC, UT, WA, WV
Required to Follow Existing Political Subdivisions (20 States):

AL, AR, GA, IA, ID, KS, KY, MD, MN, MO, MS, NC, NE, NH, NV, OR, SC, UT, WA, WV
Required to Preserve Communities of Interest (11 States):

AL, ID, KS, KY, MD, MN, MO, NE, OR, SC, UT
Required to Preserve Cores of Previous Districts (9 States):

AL, AR, GA, KS, KY, MD, MO, NC, SC
Subject to Voting Rights Act Preclearance (12 States):[1]

AL, AZ, CA, FL, GA, LA, MS, NC, NY, SC, TX, VA

SOURCES: Voting and Democracy Research Center (2004); U.S. Department of Justice, Civil Rights Division (2008).
[1] Prior to 2013.

2004). These impose a considerable constraint on the ability of legislators to use redistricting to further partisan goals through gerrymandering.

Beyond compactness, state constitutions often impose additional constraints on the redistricting process. Table 1.1 also summarizes these constraints: nineteen states require that congressional districts be contiguous; twenty also require that the district boundaries follow as near as possible existing county, city, and other municipal boundaries; eleven require redistricting plans to avoid splitting apart communities of interest, such as racial and ethnic neighborhoods; and nine states also require that redrawn congressional districts preserve the cores of prior districts, thus mandating that previous electoral boundaries be left at least somewhat intact (Voting and Democracy Research Center 2004). While contiguity requirements are not expected to impose much of a constraint on partisan gerrymandering, the need to protect either existing political subdivisions or avoid splitting communities of interest can, depending on the patterns of population concentration and dispersion of partisan voters within those subdivisions and communities, pose a significant obstacle for the twin gerrymandering strategies of cracking and packing. Requirements that plans preserve the cores of previous congressional districts prevent redistricters from radically altering the electoral landscape in pursuit of partisan advantage, and therefore will have the effect of biasing redistricting in favor of preserving the status quo.

One Person, One Vote

One of the central questions in redistricting and reapportionment litigation since the middle of the twentieth century has been the extent to which districts within a state legislative or congressional redistricting plan must have exactly— or as near to it as practically possible—equal populations. Significant malapportionment in legislative districts had arisen prior to the Supreme Court's involvement in this issue, as states often failed to redraw their districts at all in response to changes in their population distribution, often resulting in significant overrepresentation of rural areas at the expense of expanding urban centers. Beginning with the landmark case of *Baker v. Carr* (1962), the Supreme Court relaxed its political question doctrine in a way that for the first time allowed it to enter the "political thicket" of redistricting and reapportionment-related litigation. Two years later, in *Wesberry v. Sanders* and its companion case, *Reynolds v. Sims* (1964), the Supreme Court began to mandate increasingly strict standards of population equality in redistricting plans in order to avoid a finding of an unconstitutional Equal Protection Clause violation under the Fourteenth Amendment.

This constitutional requirement of "one person, one vote" (originally, "one man, one vote") has acted as a significant constraint on partisan gerrymandering.

Redistricters must strive for almost absolute equality in district populations in order to avoid the scrutiny of the federal courts, which have tended to frown on partisan redistricting plans with even relatively minor population deviations. In *Karcher v. Daggett* (1983), the Supreme Court struck down an attempted political gerrymander by Democrats in New Jersey, ruling that the population deviation of just under 1 percent between the smallest and largest districts, whereby the largest district contained 3,674 more people than the smallest, was unconstitutional because it did not represent a "good-faith effort to achieve population equality." This represented the first time in the court's history that it struck down a reapportionment plan with an average and maximum population variance of under 1 percent. The decision is notable in that it categorically rejected any notion that an attempt to benefit one political party over another could represent a legitimate state interest in the redistricting process, thus signaling the intent of the federal courts to apply greater scrutiny to redistricting plans that deviated even slightly from population equality in the pursuit of partisan advantage.

In subsequent cases, the federal courts also struck down a Republican gerrymander of congressional districts in Pennsylvania on the basis of a just a nineteen-person population difference between the largest and smallest districts (*Vieth v. Pennsylvania*, 2002), and a similar Democratic gerrymander of state house and senate districts in Georgia (*Larios v. Cox*, 2004). The Supreme Court's "one person, one vote" precedent therefore constrains the extent to which those in control of redistricting can manipulate population deviations between districts to achieve partisan goals, and the court's explicit rejection of partisan advantage as a legitimate state interest has meant that it has generally applied higher standards of constitutional scrutiny to redistricting plans that contain obvious partisan gerrymandering.

Voting Rights Act Preclearance

The enactment of the Voting Rights Act (VRA) in 1965 and its subsequent renewals in 1970, 1975, 1982, and 2006, in addition to representing a significant step forward in outlawing the disenfranchisement of minority voters through racial discrimination in voter registration, ushered in a new era of affirmative action in the redistricting process. The act, as broadly interpreted by the Justice Department and the federal courts, requires states to use the redistricting process to defend and enhance the rights of minority voters to elect candidates of their choice through the creation of majority-minority districts: districts where a particular minority group represents a majority of the voting-age population. Section 5 of the act also requires that any changes in electoral regulations in areas with a history of minority disenfranchisement be submitted to the Department of Justice (DOJ) or the federal courts for preclearance before they are allowed to take effect. The Section 5 preclearance requirements applied mostly to jurisdictions in the South, including the states of Alabama, Alaska, Arizona, Georgia, Louisiana, Mississippi, South Carolina, Texas, and parts of Virginia. Its application to select counties in California, Florida, Illinois, New Hampshire, New York, and South Dakota also subjected proposed redistricting plans in those states to the preclearance requirements of Section 5. Despite the significant improvements in minority voting rights and representation that have taken place since the 1960s (between 1965 and 1974, 5.5 percent of proposed changes were objected to by the DOJ, whereas this decreased to 1.2 percent between 1975 and 1982, 0.6 percent between 1983 and 2004, and less than 0.1 percent since 2005), Section 5 remains in effect for these jurisdictions until at least 2031, its temporary provisions having been renewed in 2006 for an additional twenty-five years. In order to be eligible for preclearance, those responsible for redistricting in Section 5 jurisdictions must demonstrate that the challenged plan not only does not discriminate on the basis of race but also is not in any way retrogressive to minority voting rights. However, in the 2013 case of *Shelby County v. Holder*, the Supreme Court declared the coverage formula for Section 5 preclearance, contained in Section 4 of the VRA, to be an unconstitutional burden on the covered states since it was based on "40 year old facts having no relation to the present day." Twelve states were required to submit their redistricting plans to the Justice Department for preclearance during the redistricting cycles in the 1990s and 2000s, as they were either completely or partially covered by Section 5. The applicability of Section 5 moving forward will be determined when and if Congress passes legislation establishing a new coverage formula, or through the use of Section 3 of the VRA to "bail-in" jurisdictions through the federal courts.

The requirements of the Voting Rights Act therefore can constrain redistricting in two ways. First, redistricters are required to create majority-minority districts in order to enhance minority representation, a process that can decrease the effectiveness of the optimal partisan gerrymander, especially in the presence of geographical constraints and supermajority-minority mandates (Shotts 2001). In redrawing district boundaries, states are thus attempting to balance two competing guarantees: one derived from the Voting Rights Act, which mandates that no state may dilute the voting strength of racial minorities, and the other from the Fourteenth Amendment of the Constitution, as interpreted by the U.S. Supreme Court, which requires that no state may discriminate on the basis of race. The constitutional quandary raised by the creation of majority-minority districts is that in order to prevent vote dilution, states must resort to a form of discrimination. States must take race into account when conducting redistricting in order to comply with the Voting Rights Act, but in order to comply with the Fourteenth Amendment, they cannot explicitly redraw districts on the basis of race. The Supreme Court's solution to this problem—that states can take race into account when drawing majority-minority districts, but it cannot be the "predominant factor" (*Shaw v. Reno*, 509 U.S. 630 (1993); *Miller v. Johnson*, 515 U.S. 900 (1995); *Bush v. Vera*, 517 U.S. 952 (1996))—has resulted in district boundaries being redrawn by the courts on a number of occasions where partisan gerrymandering may have been implemented in the absence of this constraint.

Second, at least in theory, in order to secure DOJ preclearance, redistricters also bear the burden of proof to demonstrate that the challenged plan does not adversely affect minority voting rights, including, as broadly defined, any splitting of a district in which a minority group constitutes a majority of the population. This becomes particularly difficult to achieve through redistricting where a state has seen a decline in its minority population over time, or where that population is not significantly concentrated geographically. In such situations, it becomes extremely burdensome for the state to maintain the existing quota of majority-minority districts, and attempts to implement partisan gerrymandering under these circumstances have often fallen afoul of the preclearance process and subsequent challenges in the federal courts (Monmonier 2001).

Structural Constraints on Redistricting

The ability to manipulate election results using redistricting is also affected by the way the legislature itself is structured. Variables such as the number of legislative seats, the ways in which they are allocated between states, and the electoral realignment created by previous redistricting cycles all can impose structural barriers that undermine the ability to gerrymander effectively.

Congressional Reapportionment

After each decennial census, seats in the House of Representatives are reapportioned to reflect changes in state populations in the intervening years. With the total number of House seats remaining at around 435 since the early twentieth century (it briefly expanded to 437 with the admission of Alaska and Hawaii in 1959, but reverted to 435 after the 1960 Census, where it has remained), this inevitably results in some states with decreasing population losing seats and other states with increasing population gaining seats. The 2000 Census, for example, saw twelve congressional seats reapportioned: Arizona, Florida, Georgia, and Texas each gained two seats, while California, Colorado, Nevada, and North Carolina each gained one. New York and Pennsylvania each lost two seats, whereas Connecticut, Illinois, Indiana, Michigan, Mississippi, Ohio, Oklahoma, and Wisconsin each lost one. The net regional change reflected a movement in population from the Northeast and Midwest (which each lost five seats) to the South (which gained seven and lost two) and to the West (which gained five) (Mills 2001). It is considerably easier to implement a partisan gerrymander in a state that has gained seats as a result of reapportionment than it is in a state that has lost seats, so controlling the redistricting process in these states can yield much greater rewards in terms of partisan advantage than controlling redistricting in states that have lost seats or where there has been no change. Any additional seats gained from reapportionment can almost always be integrated into a new set of boundaries that can be drawn to practically ensure that the party controlling redistricting will capture those seats, meaning that any seats gained by a state through reapportionment are very likely to be reflected in the win total of that party in the next election. Reapportionment also generally requires a much more extensive redrawing of electoral boundaries than population migration alone, due to laws that mandate standards such as compactness, contiguity, and preserving the cores of previous districts.

The in-party may take advantage of these factors to gerrymander far more extensively when the state has gained seats than they might have been able to do without reapportionment. Conversely, in states that either lose seats or have no change in their congressional representation, implementing effective partisan gerrymandering is considerably more difficult, and the vast majority of states fall into this second category. The 2000 redistricting cycle is a case in point: of the twenty-four congressional districts that the party controlling redistricting was able to capture in the subsequent election, seven were in states that gained representation in Congress as a result of reapportionment, whereas just four were in states that had lost seats in Congress.

Number of Districts

Gilligan and Matsusaka (1999) demonstrate that the ability for partisan control of redistricting to bring about significant partisan bias in subsequent elections is dependent on structural features of the partisan environment, such as the size of the voting population and the number of districts within a jurisdiction. This is clearly an important issue for congressional redistricting, as the number of districts in a U.S. House delegation can vary significantly from state to state. The authors uncover evidence that both the voting population and the number of districts have a conditional effect on the relationship between control of redistricting, measured indirectly using the Ranney index of party strength (Ranney 1965), and overall partisan bias in state congressional delegations. As state voting population increases, the effect of party strength on partisan bias is magnified, whereas an increase in the number of congressional seats in a state delegation has a mitigating effect on the relationship.

The reason for this is that each seat captured by a party through gerrymandering in a small state exerts a larger substantive effect on the overall level of partisan bias than a corresponding seat captured through redistricting in a large state. Though the populations of congressional districts within states must follow a constitutional mandate of population equality, congressional apportionment can produce somewhat varying district populations between states, differences that can be further exacerbated over time due to population migration. For example, based on data from the National Conference of State Legislatures redistricting project, following congressional reapportionment as a result of the 2000 Census, the ideal district populations in states with at least two congressional seats ranged from 524,000 (Rhode Island) to 744,000 (Utah), with a mean of 643,500 and a standard deviation of 37,000. Partisan redistricting is therefore constrained by the size of a state's congressional delegation, and may decline in effectiveness over time in response to changes in the size and distribution of a state's voting population.

Existing Political Alignment

When studying the effects of partisan control of redistricting on subsequent elections, it is tempting to treat the redistricting process itself as exogenous: an outside influence on elections whose effects do not depend on previous electoral conditions. In reality, however, the ability of partisan gerrymandering to produce significant partisan effects in subsequent elections is in many ways dependent on the level of bias in the elections prior to gerrymandering. The 2003 Republican redistricting in Texas is an ideal illustration of this. Critics focused on the plan because of the dramatic seat changes it produced in the 2004 election, where the Republicans captured six seats previously controlled by the Democrats. Yet the reason why so many districts changed hands was that the existing electoral alignment prior to redistricting had significantly favored the Democratic Party. In another example, though the Democrats controlled redistricting in California in 2001, the fact that the political alignment in that state was already in their favor meant that they were unable to increase their seat total in 2002 aside from winning the single district that was added to the California delegation as a result of reapportionment. The most important questions to answer, then, are: under what electoral conditions are we most likely to see partisan gerrymandering occur, and what would we expect the consequences of these conditions to be for the subsequent effectiveness of the gerrymander?

Redistricting itself is not conducted in a vacuum. A party in control of the redistricting process must operate not only within the constraints of what they are realistically able to achieve but also what they have achieved in the past. Partisan gerrymandering can only occur where one party controls all branches of state government. It is likely that, in such a state, the party will also control a considerable portion of that state's congressional delegation. In cases where a party already controls most of the congressional districts in a state, it is unlikely that it will be able to make an appreciable gain in representation through redistricting. In the most extreme example, it is impossible for a party to capture seats through redistricting if it already holds all the seats to begin with, as the Democrats currently do in the state of Massachusetts. Though this situation is rare, generally any party that is able to gain unilateral control of redistricting in a state is also likely to be well represented in that state's congressional delegation, and so has less to gain from partisan gerrymandering.

Conversely, gerrymandering has the greatest potential to produce partisan effects in states whose prior electoral boundaries had significantly disadvantaged the party now in control of redistricting. Texas is an example of this: the Republicans were able to gain so many seats from their 2003 redistricting because the electoral map had been so thoroughly tilted against them under the previous set of boundaries. The most fertile climate for an effective partisan gerrymander of congressional districts, therefore, would seem to be a state where a party that was significantly disadvantaged by the existing configuration of congressional districts is then able to gain unified partisan control of the state government at the time of the present redistricting. This would seem to indicate a situation where a party's growing strength in state elections has not yet been translated into a gain in congressional seats by the time of reapportionment. The likelihood of such a situation occurring, notwithstanding the example of Texas, is reduced by the fact that the disadvantaged party must be able to overcome any disadvantage in state elections in order to subsequently control the redrawing of the congressional boundaries. To summarize: the circumstances in which partisan gerrymandering is likely to be most effective are also the circumstances in which it is least likely to occur.

Geographical Constraints on Redistricting

At its most basic level, redistricting involves the allocation of individual voters into the aggregate and artificial geographic units we know as legislative districts.

If the American population were randomly distributed in geographical space according to their stated partisanship, then political gerrymandering could not exist: every district would have the same alignment of Democrats, Republicans, and Independents. Instead, it relies on taking advantage of the nonrandom geographical distribution of voters to combine populations of interest in a way that alters subsequent election outcomes. These geographical patterns however, can also place obstacles in the way of a party attempting to implement an effective gerrymander.

Population Concentration and Dispersion

Any attempt to implement an effective partisan gerrymander through the redistricting process is necessarily constrained by the patterns of concentration and dispersion of partisan voters within the target jurisdiction. A key strategy in any gerrymander is to pack certain blocs of voters into districts where they constitute a large majority, thus resulting in a significant number of wasted votes, while cracking other blocs of voters into more competitive districts where fewer votes are wasted. The result of this is that the geographical distribution of a target population significantly affects potential districting solutions designed to either minimize or maximize that population's level of representation, with the utility of a packing approach dictated by the extent to which these targeted voting blocs are geographically concentrated (Shotts 2001).

In the context of racial gerrymandering, the degree to which a racial group is geographically segregated from the white population has significant implications for the level of minority representation that is achievable through redistricting. Whereas residential integration makes manipulating minority representation more difficult, the maximum potential for minority representation is significantly higher where residential segregation is pronounced (Rogerson and Yang 1999). The same logic can be applied to partisan gerrymandering, where the ability of one party to use redistricting to gain an electoral advantage over another party is dependent on the extent to which the supporters of the targeted party are geographically segregated from those of the gerrymandering party. Where supporters of both parties are geographically dispersed throughout the electoral landscape, it becomes increasingly difficult to manipulate the district boundaries to either pack or crack supporters of one party, especially when facing additional geographical constraints such as contiguity, compactness, and the need to preserve communities of interest or to follow existing political subdivisions. Though there is some evidence that supporters of the Democratic and Republican Parties in the United States tend to be clustered in particular areas of electoral strength (Gimpel and Schuknecht 2003), in states where partisans are geographically dispersed to some degree, this acts as a constraint on the extent to which partisan redistricting can be utilized to affect subsequent electoral outcomes.

Population Migration

A second geographical constraint stems from the residential mobility of populations of voters that redistricting seeks to assign to the geographical units of congressional districts, as well as other changes in the partisan composition of the electorate that may occur over time. The problem for a party attempting to implement a long-term partisan gerrymander is that district boundaries are static, whereas the populations they attempt to manipulate are dynamic and constantly shifting. Any electoral coalition created by targeted redistricting, especially the necessarily marginal majorities required to implement an effective partisan gerrymander, are likely to erode over time as populations and voting blocs shift and change due to migration, immigration, and generational replacement. Over time, the populations of different congressional districts can potentially change to such an extent that a state's population can differ dramatically from its original size and distribution at the time of the most recent census, thus confounding the original intent of a redistricting plan.

According to estimates derived from the American Community Survey (ACS), by 2006, the largest congressional district had a population of almost 950,000 people, whereas the smallest had a population of just over 390,000. In terms of population change, the survey estimated that the fastest-growing district increased its population by more than 300,000 between 2000 and 2006, whereas the district with the most rapidly declining population lost approximately 245,000 people over the same period. Arizona's Sixth District, which contains many of the eastern suburbs of the city of Phoenix, was both the fastest growing and the largest as of 2006. Louisiana's Second District, which contains most of the city of New Orleans and some of its suburbs, was both the smallest and experienced the largest population decline. These obviously represent extreme cases—the dramatic population decline in Louisiana was a direct result of the destruction caused by Hurricane Katrina, whereas Maricopa County in Arizona is one of the fastest-growing areas of the country. Nevertheless, there were sixteen congressional districts that experienced a growth in population of more than 150,000 from 2000 to 2006, and eighteen districts that experienced a decline of more than 25,000 over the same time span. The mean absolute net population change for all congressional districts from 2000 to 2006 was approximately 48,000.

It is clear, therefore, that significant population migration can take place in the years between decennial censuses and, toward the end of the decade, the congressional district boundaries may represent very different populations than they did when they were drawn. Since the intention of partisan gerryman-dering is to maximize vote efficiency, thereby capturing the maximum number of seats with the fewest number of votes, it often produces an electoral majority based on victories in a significant number of marginal seats. These seats may become increasingly difficult to hold on to in subsequent elections, especially if population migration produces an influx of voters who identify with the opposing party. Even politically neutral migration patterns can potentially have a significant effect on vote efficiency in instances where it modifies the existing population alignment. There is a great potential for artificial electoral majorities created by gerrymandering to erode over time due to population shifts that alter the partisan composition of the electorate. While redistricters may attempt to predict future population trends based on extrapolations from past data, the inherent uncertainty of these estimates and the necessity of sacrificing immediate partisan gains to ac-count for possible future developments make this a risky strategy to pursue.

The Effects of Redistricting

The process of redrawing political boundaries in response to each decennial census is one that operates under a significant number of constraints. Redistrict-ers, far from being free to indulge their partisan, political, or personal goals and impose any configuration of boundaries that suits their needs, must instead work within the political, institutional, structural, and geographical constraints that are inherent in the way that the redistricting process is conducted in the United States. What, then, are the implications of these constraints, both for ex-pectations about the effects of redistricting on subsequent election outcomes and for potential differences between various redistricting methods in terms of their goals and anticipated impact? One implication is that the effects of redis-tricting are conditional—a certain combination of circumstances must be pres-ent in order for control of the redrawing of district boundaries to fundamentally affect subsequent election outcomes. This leads to two observable implications that can be empirically tested.

First, a party in control of the redistricting process cannot always use that control to systematically tilt the electoral playing field in its favor: we would ex-pect to find significant partisan effects under some circumstances but not others, and the net impact of redistricting on partisan advantage and bias is expected to be minimal. Chapters 2 and 3 frame a preliminary test for this hypothesis by focusing on the states that have been at issue in the Supreme Court's recent partisan gerrymandering cases. Detailed analysis of subsequent election results in these states reveals no evidence of long-lasting electoral effects, providing preliminary evidence in support of the court's conclusions. The extent to which the constrained nature of redistricting can mitigate the degree to which partisan gerrymandering can introduce pervasive and long-lasting bias into a state's congressional delegation is addressed in more detail in Chapter 4, which subjects hypotheses about the effects of redistricting on electoral disproportionality to rigorous empirical testing.

Second, when considering the potential impact of redistricting on variables such as competitiveness and electoral responsiveness, it is evident that the most important factor to take into account is not necessarily who *controls* redistricting, but what the *intent* of a particular redistricting plan is. Redistricting plans that focus on protecting the electoral strength of incumbents are expected to reduce electoral competitiveness, whereas plans that focus on explicitly partisan goals are expected to increase it.

THE UNREALIZED PRECEDENT OF *DAVIS V. BANDEMER*

The involvement of the U.S. Supreme Court in what to many is "the most political of processes," the rules and regulations that determine how citizens elect their representatives at all levels of government, has been a contentious one from its very inception (Epstein 2002). The court's decision in the landmark case of *Baker v. Carr* (1962) to intervene in an area of public policy, which to that point had always been considered a nonjusticiable political question, was one of the most arduous and gut-wrenching in its history. The case exposed the deep internal divisions in jurisprudence between the liberal activist wing of the court led by Justice William Brennan and Chief Justice Earl Warren, and the "allies on judicial self-restraint," Justices John Harlan and Felix Frankfurter (O'Brien 2005). Since that time, the Supreme Court has handed down numerous decisions concerning election law, delving deeper into the "political thicket" that Frankfurter had cautioned against entering. The more conservative Burger Court showed no less willingness toward involvement in this area than the liberal Warren Court, effectively establishing the federal judiciary as a final review body for the electoral practices of federal, state, and local government (O'Brien 2005, 823–31). Even the Rehnquist and Roberts Courts, with their emphasis on judicial restraint and frequent attempts to roll back the perceived excesses of previous activist eras, have proven themselves "willing to weigh in on virtually any aspect of election law, with often dramatic consequences" (Epstein 2002).

This point is illustrated no better than in the case of *Bush v. Gore* (2000), where for the first time in its history, the Supreme Court intervened to settle a dispute over the outcome of a presidential election. The court has handed down landmark decisions in the areas of campaign finance regulations (*Buckley v. Valeo* (1976), *Colorado Republican Federal Campaign Committee v. FEC* (1996), *McConnell v. FEC* (2003), *Citizens United v. FEC* (2010)), primary election voting requirements (*California Democratic Party v. Jones* (2000)), and racial redistricting (*Shaw v. Reno (Shaw I)* (1993)), *Miller v. Johnson* (1995)). Why, then, has there been so little Supreme Court case law on the issue of partisan gerrymandering, and so little agreement among the justices as to how to approach it?

Relevant Precedents

Badham v. Eu was the first case before the federal courts in the years after *Davis v. Bandemer* to wrestle with the practical applications of the plurality opinion's two-prong test for unconstitutional political gerrymandering (694 F. Supp. 664 (N.D. Cal. 1988), summarily affirmed, 488 U.S. 1024 (1989)). Most scholars who have focused on this case have criticized the court for reiterating the two-prong test, which they argue set impossibly high standards for any challenge to a partisan gerrymander to meet (Capobianco 1988; Crouch 1987; Grofman 1990). Comparatively little attention, however, has been paid to *Badham*'s most significant holding: that the *Bandemer* precedent, which had initially been applied to the drawing of state legislative districts only, also extends to the drawing of congressional districts (Note 2004).

The *Badham* case arose from the redrawing of California's congressional districts in the aftermath of the 1980 census, which saw the state increase its seats in the House of Representatives from forty-three to forty-five. The previous district boundaries, which had been drawn by the California Supreme Court in 1973 after then governor Ronald Reagan failed to reach an agreement with the Democratically-controlled state legislature, had resulted in Californians electing twenty-two Republicans and twenty-one Democrats to the House in the 1980 election. The Democrats, now in control of both houses of the legislature and the governorship, proceeded to pass a new redistricting plan that sought to maximize Democratic representation in Congress. However, this plan was struck down via ballot initiative in the June 1982 primary election. Nevertheless, the California Supreme Court ordered that the challenged districts must be used for the 1982 congressional election since no other viable alternative existed, and as a result, the Democrats were able to capture a 28–17 advantage in California's House delegation, although the Democratic candidate was defeated in the state's gubernatorial election. Shortly before leaving office, outgoing Democratic governor Jerry Brown called a special session of the state legislature to pass a new reapportionment bill, allegedly heavily based on the previously rejected boundaries, which the governor signed into law on his final day in office. Republicans challenged the plan in both state and federal courts, and after dismissing this earlier complaint, the district court agreed to rehear the petition in light of the Supreme Court's decision in *Davis v. Bandemer* (see 694 F. Supp. 666).

The plaintiffs alleged that the Democratic plan represented an unconstitutional political gerrymander under *Bandemer*'s two-prong test, in that it diluted the voting strength of Republicans in California. The district court, addressing the merits of the claim, had no difficulty accepting the charge under *Bandemer*'s first prong, observing that "as an initial matter, it is clear that the complaint sufficiently alleges a discriminatory intent" (694 F. Supp. 669). However, they concluded that there was no evidence of "consistent degradation of Republican influence of the political process as a whole" (Note 2004, 1207). In fact, according to the court, "California Republicans represent so potent a political force that it is unnecessary for the judiciary to intervene," to the extent that "it would simply be ludicrous for plaintiffs to allege that their interests are being entirely ignore[d]" (694 F. Supp. 672). On the issue of justiciability, the district court found that "nothing in *Bandemer*'s ... analysis ... turn[ed] on the distinction between congressional redistricting and state legislative redistricting," and so they had no problem extending the precedent to cases involving congressional district boundries (694 F. Supp. 668).

On appeal, the Supreme Court summarily affirmed the district court's holding and, in doing so, effectively extended *Bandemer*'s two-prong test to cover congressional elections as well as those for state legislatures. An examination of lower court political gerrymandering decisions in the wake of *Badham* reveals that this is exactly the standard the courts have applied across the board, and so with little fanfare, the Supreme Court's summary affirmance effectively established *Bandemer* as the law of the land. In considering a challenge to a partisan gerrymander in the state of North Carolina in the case of *Pope v. Blue* (809 F. Supp. 392 (W.D. N.C. 1992), summarily affirmed, 506 U.S. 801 (1992)), the district court stated that "due in particular to the fact that the *Bandemer* Court was unable to agree on a majority opinion, we believe that the *Badham* court's interpretation of *Bandemer,* subsequently summarily affirmed by the Supreme Court, is entitled to substantial deference" (809 F. Supp. 395). This also has been the approach taken by other federal courts when addressing the merits of subsequent political gerrymandering claims, and several of these rulings also have been summarily affirmed by the Supreme Court (under 28 U.S.C. § 2284(a), cases involving challenges to the constitutionality of the apportionment of congressional or state legislative districts are heard before a special three-judge district court panel, with the statute also providing for mandatory Supreme Court appellate review).

Because the two-prong political gerrymandering test in *Bandemer* was established by a plurality opinion rather than an actual majority, it was not binding on the court or the rest of the federal judiciary under the doctrine of stare decisis, even though, as the previously cited cases demonstrate, lower federal courts have often elected to apply it. As the plurality in *Vieth v. Jubelirer* (541 U.S. 267 (2004)) noted, "*stare decisis* does not require that *Bandemer* be allowed to stand. *Stare decisis* claims are weakest with respect to a decision interpreting the Constitution, particularly where there has been no reliance on that decision." The Supreme Court's precedent on political gerrymandering was therefore a shaky one from its very inception, and at no point was there ever a majority of justices willing to declare political gerrymandering unconstitutional under a definitive constitutional standard.

Additional light may be shed on this point by examining the ideological leanings of the justices themselves. It is true that two of the three members of the court who were present for both *Bandemer* and *Vieth*, Chief Justice William Rehnquist and Justice Sandra Day O'Connor, were part of the minority of three who opposed declaring justiciability, with only Justice John Paul Stevens voting in favor; however, Stevens remains the only member of the court present in all three political gerrymandering cases. Of the five justices who voted to declare political gerrymandering justiciable in 1986 who have subsequently left the court—Justices Byron White, William Brennan, Thurgood Marshall, Harry Blackmun, and Lewis Powell—three were replaced by nominees of Republican presidents: Anthony Kennedy was nominated by Ronald Reagan, and both David Souter and Clarence Thomas were nominated by George H. W. Bush. The nominations by George W. Bush of John Roberts and Samuel Alito each replace justices who voted to overrule *Bandemer*, and so do not seem likely to significantly affect the balance of power on this issue. Similarly, Barack Obama's appointment of Sonia Sotomayor and Elena Kagan to the court is also unlikely to shift the balance of power, as they replace Justices Souter and Stevens, respectively, each of whom voted to strike down the challenged plan in both *Vieth* and the subsequent case of *LULAC v. Perry* (548 U.S. 399 (2006)). It is clear, however, that the ideological makeup of the court has shifted significantly since 1986, and given that these changes began so soon after the case was decided, with the promotion of Rehnquist to chief justice and the appointment of Antonin Scalia as associate justice, it is not surprising that the court was reluctant to revisit the issue for so many years.

Although the precedent of the two-prong test for unconstitutional political gerrymandering established by the plurality opinion in *Bandemer* has been the law of the land for more than two decades, aside from the summary affirmance in *Badham,* the Supreme Court did not hear another case on the issue until some eighteen years after *Bandemer* was decided. The conventional wisdom held by many at the time was that *Bandemer* failed to generate a slew of political gerrymandering litigation before the Supreme Court because the decision itself was hopelessly vague and failed to enunciate "a coherent theory of constitutional adjudication of partisan gerrymandering claims" (Grofman 1990). However, some have argued that the decision did establish definitive standards for adjudicating cases that may subsequently arise after the declaration of justiciability, but these standards were simply so high as to invalidate the vast majority of claims. Some have even alleged that Justice White's standard was excessively stringent to the point that it led to an erroneous conclusion in the case (Crouch 1987).

An examination of the application of the *Bandemer* precedent by the lower federal courts in the two decades since reveals a remarkable amount of consistency that, far from indicating that the opinion was incomprehensively vague, in fact demonstrates that the lower courts have been able to apply it extremely effectively (Lowenstein 2005). Of the eighteen gerrymanders that have been challenged in the federal courts under the *Bandemer* precedent since 1986, the gerrymander was upheld in all but one. The one exception is the case of *Republican Party of North Carolina v. Martin* (1992), which struck down North Carolina's statewide system of electing superior court judges, a system that had resulted in the election of only one Republican judge since 1900. Not only did this case arguably misapply the *Bandemer* precedent since it did not involve the drawing of district lines, but just five days after the district court announced its decision and concluded that the statewide method of electing judges "had resulted in Republican candidates experiencing a consistent and pervasive lack of success and exclusion from the electoral process as a whole and that these effects were likely to continue unabated into the future," the Republican Party won every contested seat in the elections for superior court judgeships (Kang 2005). On appeal, and finding this result to be "directly at odds with the recent prediction by the district court," the Fourth Circuit Court of Appeals overruled the decision in *Republican Party of North Carolina v. Hunt* (1996).

The subsequent lower court decisions that have attempted to apply the *Bandemer* precedent have therefore found little evidence of effects that were severe or long-lasting enough stemming from partisan redistricting to meet the second prong of the court's constitutional standard. In the 2004 case of *Vieth v. Jubelirer,* the court would confront the question of whether or not to entirely abandon this judicial foray into partisan gerrymandering jurisprudence.

A Court Divided

The circumstances surrounding the *Vieth* case differ slightly from those at issue in *Bandemer* because the alleged political gerrymander in *Vieth* concerned the reapportionment plan for the congressional districts in the state of Pennsylvania rather than those for the state assembly. The case is similar in that respect to *Badham*, which also involved congressional districts; however, the *Vieth* case involved a challenge to a Republican political gerrymander rather than a Democratic one. Following congressional reapportionment after the 2000 Census, Pennsylvania lost two of its twenty-one representatives in the House. The reason for this reduction in representation was changes in population over the ten-year period since the previous census, which had seen the total population of the state reduced by around twenty thousand (Mills 2001). This was part of a long-term trend in which states in the Northeast and Midwest have lost population, and as a result representation, to southern and western states.

The task of redrawing the boundaries of Pennsylvania's nineteen remaining congressional districts is the responsibility of the state legislature. At the time the redistricting plan was being drawn up, the Republicans happened to have majorities in both houses of the state legislature, as well as control of the governorship, effectively giving them free rein to implement any partisan gerrymander they wished. The subsequent plan, which was passed by the state legislature in 2002, made use of "new advances in voter databases, mapping, and other computer technologies," to ensure the maximum number of Republican members of Congress (Lazarus 2003). Prior to the redistricting, the Pennsylvania congressional delegation had consisted of eleven Republicans and ten Democrats, and the state was generally evenly split between Democrats and Republicans. Democratic presidential candidates Al Gore and John Kerry each won the state with 51 percent of the vote, and a breakdown of registered voters shows a relatively even split between the two parties.

Many of the complaints leveled at the Pennsylvania plan are similar to those raised in *Bandemer,* in that the plan failed to reasonably or reliably follow existing county, city, or even township boundaries. At issue in *Vieth* was whether the plan was unconstitutional on the basis of population, with the plaintiffs alleging that the nineteen-person population difference between the largest and smallest districts violated the constitutional principle of "one person, one vote" under Article I, Section 2 of the Constitution (Brief for Appellees, 2002 U.S. Briefs 1580). Also at issue was whether the plan was unconstitutional because it violated the Equal Protection Clause of the Fourteenth Amendment, with any ruling on the merits of the equal protection claims also hinging on whether or not partisan gerrymandering challenges would still be considered a justiciable issue under the political question doctrine. After rejecting the first redistricting plan on the basis of the "one person, one vote" violations, the district court upheld a revised plan that corrected the population deviations but retained significant political gerrymandering, rejecting the Fourteenth Amendment claim of an equal protection violation. On appeal, the Supreme Court granted certiorari, and the court's opinion in *Vieth* was authored by Justice Scalia and signed by Justices Rehnquist, O'Connor, and Thomas. Justice Kennedy concurred in part with the judgment, and Justices Stevens, Souter, Stephen Breyer, and Ruth Bader Ginsburg each dissented.

Plurality Opinion—Justice Scalia

Though there were five votes on the Supreme Court to dismiss the claim of an unconstitutional political gerrymander, only a plurality of four votes existed to declare the issue a nonjusticiable political question, consisting of Justices Scalia, Rehnquist, O'Connor, and Thomas. Justice Scalia's justification in his plurality opinion was the lack of judicially discoverable and manageable standards for resolving the claim. In effect, the plurality concluded that political gerrymandering must be nonjusticiable because no effective standards exist to adjudicate whether such a claim is unconstitutional or not. The plurality would have overruled *Bandemer,* arguing that the previous case had "held that political gerrymandering claims are justiciable, but could not agree upon a standard for assessing [them]" (541 U.S. 271–2). Scalia notes that in the intervening years, no alleged political gerrymanders had passed the two-prong test for "intentional discrimination against an identifiable political group and an actual discriminatory effect on that group." He concludes that "eighteen years of judicial effort with virtually nothing to show for it justifies revisiting" whether the precedent should be upheld (281).

A great deal of criticism has been leveled at Scalia's opinion in this case. The major problem with his approach to the justiciability question—that partisan gerrymandering must be a political question because of a lack of judicially discoverable manageable standards for adjudicating it—is that in advancing this claim, he necessarily attempts to prove a negative. While it is easy to argue that no such standards have yet been developed, it is much more difficult to contend that one does not exist, and that no workable standard could ever "distinguish an unconstitutional partisan gerrymander from a permissible districting plan" (Lowenstein 2005). Furthermore, he supports this argument by highlighting the fact that not one political gerrymander has been struck down by the federal courts under the *Bandemer* precedent, citing this as evidence that the plurality in that case was not able to discover a manageable standard. The argument can be made, however, that because the lower courts have, in Scalia's words, "simply applied" the *Bandemer* precedent, this is evidence of exactly the opposite, and that it has in fact proven to be an extremely workable standard given the consistency with which lower federal courts have been able to implement it. Indeed, even though no case of political gerrymandering to date has been able to meet the two-prong standard, "what better proof of manageability could there be than experience showing that the standard can be and had been 'simply applied'?" (Lowenstein 2005).

While Scalia focuses his attention on this particular aspect of the political question doctrine, and attempts to support his conclusions by systematically debunking each of the standards proposed by the dissenting justices, the doctrine contains two other provisions that might arguably be better suited to the issues in this case. *Baker v. Carr* also defines controversies where "a textually demonstrable constitutional commitment of the issue to a coordinate political department" as nonjusticiable political questions (369 U.S. 217). Scalia mentions in his opinion that Article I, Section 4 gives the states responsibility for prescribing the "times, places and manner of holding elections," but reserves to Congress the right to "at any time by law make or alter such regulations." The Constitution therefore provides ample remedy for the problem of political gerrymandering to be resolved without the need for litigation, as Congress has the constitutional authority to step in at any time and pass legislation declaring the practice illegal.

However, he stops short of making the case that political gerrymandering claims should be precluded under this aspect of the political question doctrine. It would seem to be a logical extension to his argument that Article I, Section 4 represents a textually demonstrable commitment to a coordinate branch of government, and therefore is not within the purview of the federal judiciary. The advantage of this approach is that it would have respected the doctrine of stare decisis by allowing for a finding of nonjusticiability in *Vieth* without the necessity of overruling *Bandemer*. Since *Bandemer* concerned the drawing of state legislative districts rather than congressional districts, it is not governed by Article I, Section 4, although this would then raise the ancillary issue of a possible conflict with *Badham*, which extended *Bandemer*'s holding to congressional redistricting. Since *Badham* was a summary affirmation of a lower court decision, however, rather than an opinion of the Supreme Court itself, it carries much less weight under stare decisis than the *Bandemer* precedent. The political question doctrine also provides for controversies that would necessitate "an initial policy determination of a kind clearly for nonjudicial discretion" (369 U.S. 217) to be nonjusticiable and, in fact, this was the very argument that was raised in the state of Indiana's brief in *Bandemer*. This would also appear to be a superior approach to the justiciability question than Scalia's reliance on the lack of judicially manageable standards, the inherent weaknesses of which might suggest that it should be scrapped entirely.

Concurring Opinion—Justice Kennedy

In his concurring opinion, Justice Kennedy advances the interesting argument that "the First Amendment may prove to offer a sounder and more prudential basis for judicial intervention in political gerrymandering cases," drawing on the plaintiffs' claim that the freedom of association rights of the Democratic Party were being abridged (541 U.S. 315). Kennedy argues that the First Amendment provides a more appropriate standard for adjudicating claims of unconstitutional political gerrymandering than the existing two-prong Fourteenth Amendment Equal Protection test established in *Bandemer*. He contends that political gerrymandering may be unconstitutional under the First Amendment in that it "burden[s] or penalize[s] citizens because of their participation in the electoral process, their voting history, their association with a political party, or their expression of political views" (314). The advantage of this approach is that the burden of proof is significantly lower under the First Amendment than it is under the Equal Protection Clause, since "under general First Amendment principles those burdens in other contexts are unconstitutional absent a compelling government interest" (314). Nevertheless, it is difficult to draw a link between a group of voters being targeted by political gerrymandering and that same group having their representational rights excessively abridged, and, indeed, Kennedy himself concedes that "excessiveness is not easily determined" (316).

The question of whether a political gerrymander may be successfully challenged under the First Amendment therefore remains unresolved. Kennedy's stance makes him the crucial swing vote on the court on the political gerrymandering issue, and his reservations about the practice provide some encouragement to those who would like to see it outlawed. While recognizing that no judicially discernable standards yet existed for the adjudication of political gerrymandering claims, Kennedy left open the possibility that, in the future, different cases might offer up a standard that is "constitutionally satisfactory" (Dorf 2004).

Kennedy's opinion has been subject to criticism almost as widespread as that of Scalia, both from those who would like to see the court take definitive steps to outlaw political gerrymandering, and by those who would like to see the court remove itself from the issue entirely. One legal scholar charges that Kennedy's concurrence "blazed a new trail on the frontier of judicial irresponsibility" (Lowenstein 2005), in that he essentially abdicated the proper role of the judiciary by arguing that because the justices were unable to agree on a standard in their deliberations, "in the case before us, we have no standard" (541 U.S. 313).

As Scalia points out, "it is *our* job, not the plaintiffs', to explicate the standard that makes the facts alleged by the plaintiffs adequate or inadequate to state a claim. We cannot nonsuit *them* for our failure to do so" (301, emphasis in original). It is arguably Kennedy's responsibility in addressing the merits of the case to come up with a judicially manageable standard to adjudicate the controversy before the court. It is the proper role of the Supreme Court to say what the law is, not what the law is not. This highlights a shortcoming that runs throughout several of the arguments in *Vieth*. Of those who propose a standard for adjudicating political gerrymandering claims, and those who would declare the issue nonjusticiable, neither defines what it is that makes, or would make, political gerrymandering unconstitutional. It makes little sense to either search for a constitutional test or to declare that no such test exists without first defining what, if anything, you are testing for under which specific constitutional provision. Only after the constitutional issue has been framed can we then proceed to search for a judicially discernable and manageable standard for detecting and correcting constitutional violations (Briffault 2005).

Partisan Redistricting in Pennsylvania

Setting aside the legal arguments on the questions of justiciability and equal protection, the key conclusion of the justices in *Vieth* was that there was no evidence presented that the redistricting plan at issue would have a severe or long-lasting enough discriminatory effect on Democratic voters to significantly damage their future electoral prospects in the state. This conclusion can be tested by examining the available electoral evidence and, in so doing, gain some insight into the extent to which the Democratic Party has been disadvantaged in Pennsylvania elections since the Republican gerrymander was implemented. Table 2.1 shows the results of congressional elections in Pennsylvania both before and after the Republican redistricting and the *Vieth* decision.

The table reveals that prior to the Republican plan, Democrats had won an 11–10 majority in the state's congressional delegation in the elections held in 1992, 1994, 1996, and 1998, with the Republicans capturing an 11–10 majority in the 2000 election. Over the five elections held under the revised Pennsylvania reapportionment plan in 2002, 2004, 2006, 2008, and 2010, on three of the five occasions, the Republicans have been able to secure twelve of Pennsylvania's nineteen seats in the House of Representatives. Of the seven Democrats elected in 2004, five of them received more than 85 percent of the vote in their district, whereas only three of the twelve Republicans did likewise. Democrats averaged 83 percent of the vote in the seats they won, with two running un-

TABLE 2.1.   Pennsylvania Congressional Election Results, 1992–2010

YEAR	SEATS WON IN CONGRESS		% OF TWO-PARTY VOTE		AVERAGE % MARGIN OF VICTORY	
	DEM	REP	DEM	REP	DEM	REP
1992	11	10	47.9	52.1	35.2	48.0
1994	11	10	44.9	55.1	29.3	56.4
1996	11	10	52.2	47.8	33.7	24.8
1998	11	10	48.4	51.6	40.1	49.5
2000	10	11	50.6	49.4	49.8	38.7
2002	7	12	42.0	58.0	45.3	55.5
2004	7	12	49.1	50.9	69.2	41.2
2006	11	8	56.0	44.0	37.5	16.0
2008	12	7	55.4	44.6	33.2	20.5
2010	7	12	48.1	51.9	35.3	23.6

SOURCE: U.S. House of Representatives, Office of the Clerk, "Election Statistics (1920–2010)," http://clerk .house.gov/members/electionInfo/elections.html (accessed July 3, 2012).

NOTE: Average % Margin of Victory = winning party's vote % – losing party's vote %, averaged across all districts won by that party.

opposed, whereas Republicans, none of whom were unopposed, averaged just 68 percent of the vote in their districts. This is reflected in the "Margin of Victory" statistic, which has been considerably higher for the Democrats since the 2002 gerrymander, but was consistently higher for the Republicans under the previous electoral boundaries.

In the 2006 midterm election, however, the Democrats were able to capture four Republican-held seats to regain an 11–8 majority in the Pennsylvania delegation, and then in 2008, they won an additional seat, taking their share of the delegation to twelve and completely reversing the 12–7 edge that the Republicans had held just four years earlier. The 2010 Republican landslide, however, in which they gained sixty-three seats in the House overall, saw the Pennsylvania delegation shift back to a 12–7 Republican edge, reversing the gains the Democrats had made in 2006 and 2008. Taken alone, the seat division itself cannot tell us whether or not the electoral system is favoring one political party or the other, especially if the percentage of the vote is not necessarily constant. Comparing the seat division with the statewide vote division, however, may shed some light on whether or not the Republican gerrymander actually produced an electoral bias against the Democratic Party.

Contrasting the 1994 election with that of 2008, it is clear that the redistricting plan was not able to create a significant pro-Republican bias. In 1994, the Democrats received 44.9 percent of the statewide popular vote, but were able to win

52 percent of the congressional seats, indicating a low level of responsiveness to the popular vote. However, the Republicans won a very similar 44.6 percent of the vote in 2008, and yet won only 37 percent of the seats, indicating that the electoral system post-gerrymandering has been much more responsive to changes in the vote and perhaps even biased in favor of the Democrats. The Democratic margin of victory, after jumping sharply in the election immediately following redistricting, declined in the next two elections after 2004. Table 2.1 shows that in both 2002 and 2004, the Democrats actually lost the statewide popular vote, despite winning it in two of the three previous elections, while they won a significant majority of the popular vote in both 2006 and 2008. In 2010, the Republicans again won a solid majority in the statewide popular vote, which was sufficient to flip control of the House delegation. In all five elections held under the Republican plan, the party winning the statewide popular vote also won a majority of the congressional seats. The previous Democratic-drawn boundaries produced such a result only once in five elections.

Figure 2.1 plots the Democratic percentage of seats won in the Pennsylvania delegation and the Democratic share of the statewide two-party popular vote for each of the congressional elections from 1992 to 2010. It demonstrates a sharp

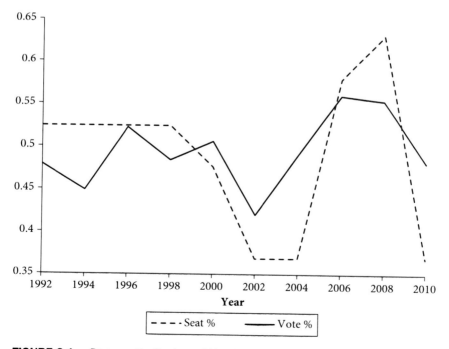

FIGURE 2.1.   Democratic Seats and Vote in Pennsylvania, 1992–2010

reversal of Democratic fortunes in the state from 1998 to 2002, followed by a dramatic growth in Democratic strength in the delegation in the following congressional elections, before the Republicans rebounded in 2010. The Republican gerrymander of 2001, while certainly improving the party's fortunes in the two subsequent elections, appears to have reversed an existing bias that was already present in the translation of votes into congressional seats in the state. The Democratic Party was able to win eleven of the state's twenty-one House seats in each of the elections from 1992 to 1998, despite receiving a majority of the statewide popular vote on only one occasion during that period, in 1996. The implementation of the Republican gerrymander coincides with a sharp decline in Democratic vote share, from a small majority in 2000 to only slightly more than 40 percent in 2002. While the Republican redistricting plan allowed them to hold on to their 12–7 seat majority in 2004 despite a nearly even split in the popular vote, the Democrats were able to secure 55 percent of the two-party vote in both 2006 and 2008, more than enough to reverse the effects of the Republican gerrymander and take back control of the state's delegation. When the national electoral climate became considerably more pro-Republican in 2010, this was also reflected in the results in Pennsylvania, demonstrating a high degree of responsiveness to changes in the overall popular vote.

Figure 2.2 presents the seats-to-votes ratio for the major political parties from 1992 to 2010, calculated by dividing their seat percentage by their percentage of the statewide popular vote. This measures the extent to which each party was overrepresented or underrepresented in each election during this period. As the graph shows, the Democratic Party was actually overrepresented in Pennsylvania's congressional delegation throughout most of the 1990s, especially in 1992 and 1994. The 1996–2000 elections saw a roughly proportional allocation of the state's House seats between the two parties, with the Democrats slightly overrepresented in 1998 and the Republicans slightly overrepresented in 2000. Following the Republican redistricting plan in the wake of the 2000 Census, there is some evidence of the gerrymander having a significant effect: the Democratic seats-to-votes ratio declined sharply in the two subsequent elections, and especially in 2004, the Democratic Party appears to be significantly underrepresented. Once again, though, it appears that the effects of the gerrymander were extremely short-lived: any inherent advantage to the Republicans in the seats-to-votes ratio had evaporated by 2006, when the Democrats actually won slightly more seats than their statewide vote percentage would suggest. By 2008, the Democrats were actually significantly overrepresented in the state delegation, picking up an additional seat even though their overall vote share actually declined slightly from 2006. This trend reverses itself in 2010, with the Republicans now overrepresented despite winning a majority of the statewide popular vote.

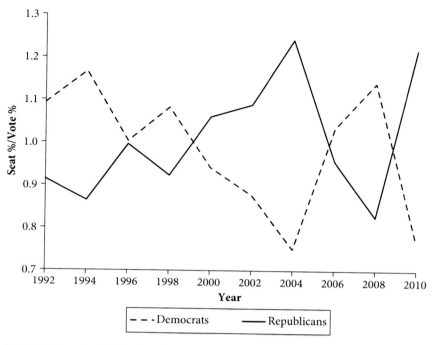

FIGURE 2.2. Seats-to-Votes Ratio in Pennsylvania, 1992–2010

The court therefore appears to have been correct in its assertion that the re-sults of only one or two elections are insufficient for making a determination as to whether an unconstitutional political gerrymander has taken place. This is why it is necessary to demonstrate a long-term discriminatory effect that entirely shuts a party out of the political process in a state before there is a chance that the court could intervene to offer relief. In the case of Pennsylvania, no such long-term electoral effects are evident, and the party that was the target of the partisan gerrymander was able to recapture enough seats to take control of the delegation by the third election following redistricting. In the following election, they actually won more congressional seats in the state then their vote percentage would seem to warrant. The alleged gerrymander in this state does not appear to have produced significant distortions in the translation of votes into seats, as the seat percentage tracks fairly closely with the two-party vote percentage both before and after the Republican gerrymander. Overall, the Republican gerrymander of 2001 seems to have injected a well-needed shot of responsiveness into U.S. House elections in the state, with the winner of the statewide popular vote capturing a majority of the House seats in each of the five subsequent elections.

One legal scholar, writing while *Vieth* was still pending before the Supreme Court, argued that "armed with the data-manipulating power of new computers, political operatives can now effectively predetermine the results of most elections," likening the practice of redistricting in the United States to Isaac Asimov's science fiction classic, the *Foundation* series, where advances in statistics allow government to predict with perfect accuracy even the most complicated human behavior (Lazarus 2003). Yet the voters of Pennsylvania were sufficiently unpredictable that the allegedly "artificial" majority created by the Republican Party through redistricting had eroded just four years and two elections after it was created. The party that was supposed to be consigned to minority status for the reminder of the decade would actually became somewhat overrepresented in the state's congressional delegation by the second half of the decade.

Another legal analyst described the court's actions in *Vieth* as "one of its most significant, and most baffling, decisions in recent history" (Toobin 2006), but as was the case with the Indiana redistricting at issue in *Bandemer,* the court appears to have been wise, on the basis of subsequent events, in avoiding a sweeping pronouncement on the constitutionality of partisan gerrymandering. Critics of the Supreme Court's decision in *Vieth* would have had the judiciary strike down the Pennsylvania plan as an unconstitutional violation of the Fourteenth Amendment Equal Protection rights of Democratic voters. This position, rejected by Justice Scalia at the time as a remedy that "the judicial department has no business entertaining" (514 U.S. 267), appears to have little evidential basis in light of the results of subsequent elections in the state.

3

SECOND-ORDER CHALLENGES AND THE RISE OF MID-DECADE REDISTRICTING

Both *Davis v. Bandemer* and *Vieth v. Jubelirer* approached the question of partisan gerrymandering of congressional boundaries through the framework of what might be called first-order equal protection review, assessing the direct effects of a challenged redistricting plan on voters' ability to elect representatives of their choice. The 2004 case of *Cox v. Larios* (300 F. Supp. 1320 (N.D. Ga. 2004), summarily affirmed, 542 U.S. 947 (2004)) demonstrates an alternative conceptual approach to the issue of political gerrymandering, one similar to that taken by the Supreme Court in the previous pre-*Bandemer* case of *Karcher v. Daggett* (1983). This approach has proven considerably more successful at striking down partisan gerrymanders than the strategy of claiming equal protection relief under the *Bandemer* precedent. The case involved the reapportionment of the Georgia state legislative and congressional districts after the 2000 Census, at which time the Democrats controlled both houses of the state legislature and the governorship. Not only did Georgia gain an additional two seats in Congress as a result of the population growth experienced by the state in the 1990s, but considerable intrastate migration had also taken place that necessitated the redrawing of the state's legislative districts as well, pursuant to Article III, Section 2 of the Georgia Constitution.

Making extensive use of voter lists and mapping software, the Georgia Democrats drew up a reapportionment plan that sought to maximize Democratic representation both in the state legislature and in the state's congressional delegation. Believing that they had a safe harbor of plus or minus 5 percent population deviation under existing "one person, one vote" standards, the legislature rejected a plan with minimal population deviation, and instead opted for one that aimed to elect the maximum possible number of Democrats, while remaining just inside the plus or minus 5 percent limit. This plan was subsequently signed into law by the Democratic governor. The house plan created a mixture of 124 single-member districts, 15 two-member districts, 6 three-member districts, and 2 four-member districts, whereas the senate plan, as dictated by Georgia law, contained exclusively single-member districts. Because Georgia is a jurisdiction covered by Section 5 of the Voting Rights Act, the state was required to have its reapportionment plans precleared by the federal government. After a series of lower federal court rulings that necessitated the revision of the Senate plan, the Supreme Court eventually upheld the revised redistricting scheme, which corrected for racial gerrymandering but retained significant partisan gerrymandering, in the case of *Georgia v. Ashcroft* (539 U.S. 461 (2003)). Georgia Republicans subsequently filed suit in federal district court to challenge the scheme under the doctrine of "one person, one vote" and *Bandemer*'s two-prong test for unconstitutional political gerrymandering.

While the district court rejected the plaintiffs' allegation of an unconstitutional political gerrymander, failing to find sufficient evidence of long-lasting discriminatory effects to satisfy *Bandemer*'s second prong, they struck down both the House and Senate plans on the basis of a violation of "one person, one vote" under the precedent of *Reynolds v. Sims* (377 U.S. 533 (1964)). The congressional plan was upheld since its population deviations were significantly smaller than those in both the House and Senate plans, and these deviations had resulted from a "legitimate effort" to conform to "easily recognizable boundaries" (300 F. Supp. 1338). Citing the "blatantly partisan and discriminatory manner" in which the scheme had been drawn up, combined with a systematic effort to use population deviations to benefit Democratic incumbents while significantly disadvantaging Republican incumbents, the district court concluded that the plans served no legitimate state interest. That the Georgia legislature exhibited discriminatory intent against Republican incumbents is hard to dispute. While only 9 of the 105 Democratic incumbents in the Georgia house and senate were paired against other incumbents, 37 of the 74 Republican incumbents were so paired, the vast majority against other Republicans. One especially unfortunate Republican incumbent senator was "drawn into a district with a Democratic incumbent . . . while an open district was drawn within two blocks of her house" (300 F. Supp. 1329–30). The Supreme Court subsequently summarily affirmed the district court's decision in a one-sentence opinion, to which Justice John Paul Stevens wrote a concurrence in which he was joined by Justice Stephen Breyer, and from which Justice Antonin Scalia dissented.

The approach taken by the courts in this case, that of second-order judicial review of political gerrymandering under "one person, one vote," has been proposed by several scholars as an alternate strategy to first-order challenges to political gerrymanders under the Equal Protection Clause. This approach has a number of advantages, most notably its considerably higher rate of success at overturning partisan gerrymanders, largely due to the lower threshold that must be met to declare a challenged plan unconstitutional under "one person, one vote." Despite the advantages of this second-order approach, however, the Supreme Court, in addressing probably the most high-profile and controversial example of partisan gerrymandering in two decades, would pass up the opportunity to extend this line of precedent in another case that came before it in 2006, one that also raised a second-order challenge to political gerrymandering.

Litigating the Perrymander

Like the Pennsylvania gerrymander at issue in *Vieth*, the case of *League of United Latin American Citizens (LULAC) v. Perry* (2006) involved the redrawing of congressional district lines by a Republican state legislature, this time in the state of Texas. As other states were losing seats in the House of Representatives due to population migration in the years between censuses, Texas experienced one of the highest population growth rates in the nation, surpassing New York as the second most populous state in the union by the year 2000. As a result of the 1990 Census, Texas gained a three-seat increase over its previous twenty-seven-seat delegation, and, in 2000, a two-seat increase brought that total to thirty-two (Mills 2001). The 2000 election saw the Republican Party controlling the governorship and the state senate, but not the state House of Representatives, and so amid deep partisan disagreement, the legislature was unable to pass a redistricting scheme that satisfied the requirements of "one person, one vote." This left the courts with the responsibility to implement a politically neutral reapportionment plan in time for the 2002 congressional election. In 2003, the Republican Party gained a majority in the state House of Representatives, and so with control of all three branches of the Texas state government, and under considerable pressure from Republicans in Congress, most notably House majority leader Tom DeLay, the Texas Republicans proceeded to redraw the congressional boundaries a second time, their stated aim being to increase Republican representation in the congressional delegation in the 2004 election.

A number of Texas Democrats immediately filed suit challenging the constitutionality of the Republican congressional district boundaries, known as Plan 1374C. The *LULAC* case differs from the court's other two partisan gerrymandering cases in that it involves an allegation of racial gerrymandering as well. In addition to challenging the constitutionality of the statewide plan, the plaintiffs also alleged that District 23 represented a racial gerrymander designed to discriminate against Latino voters. The three-judge district court panel rejected both of these claims, and the case was appealed to the Supreme Court; however, before it could be heard, the court handed down its *Vieth* opinion, and the case was remanded to the district court for reconsideration in light of the *Vieth* precedent. The district court reaffirmed its earlier decision and the case was once again appealed to the Supreme Court.

At issue in the case was whether District 23 violated Section 2 of the Voting Rights Act of 1965 because it diluted racial minority voting strength under the totality of circumstances test set by the court in *Thornburg v. Gingles* (478 U.S. 30 (1986)). Also at issue was whether the plan, being a mid-decade redistricting with the sole aim of maximizing partisan advantage, represented an unconstitutional political gerrymander that violated the "one person, one vote" requirement of the Equal Protection Clause, as it was based on 2000 Census data that no longer corresponded to the actual 2003 population distribution. In essence, the plaintiffs urged the court to strike down the Texas plan solely on the basis of its discriminatory intent, which would be sufficient to hold a partisan redistricting plan unconstitutional on the basis of "one person, one vote," without necessitating a revisiting of the illusive effects prong of the *Bandemer* constitutional test. Drawing on Justice Anthony Kennedy's opinion in *Vieth,* the plaintiffs also challenged the plan on the basis that it violated the First Amendment freedom of association, by substantially burdening a group because of its political opinions and affiliations while serving no legitimate public purpose. Justice Kennedy authored the majority opinion, in which he was joined by Justices Stevens, David Souter, Ruth Bader Ginsburg, and Stephen Breyer in ruling 5–4 that District 23 constituted an unconstitutional racial gerrymander under the *Gingles* precedent. In a separate holding, Kennedy was also joined by Justices John Roberts, Samuel Alito, Antonin Scalia, Clarence Thomas, David Souter, and Ruth Bader Ginsburg in a 7–2 ruling upholding the remainder of the Texas plan, and failing to find sufficient evidence of an unconstitutional political gerrymander on the basis of a lack of discriminatory intent.

Whereas the court's divisions in *Vieth* resulted in five separate opinions, in *LULAC,* the court produced no fewer than six opinions, and the published decision of the court runs to more than 150 pages. Justice Scalia, joined by Justice Thomas, rejected the claim of an unconstitutional racial gerrymander, and would have upheld District 23 as constitutionally permissible due to creation of the majority-minority District 25 to offset it. Justices Roberts and Alito each rejected the finding of an unconstitutional racial gerrymander, and concurred in the holding that Texas's mid-decade redistricting was constitutional, but declined to revisit the justiciability question. Justices Stevens and Breyer would have found the Texas plan to be an unconstitutional partisan gerrymander under the *Bandemer* precedent, and Justices Souter and Ginsburg would have remanded the case to the district court to reconsider the racial gerrymandering issue under more precise direction from the Supreme Court. Although Kennedy's majority opinion declined to reconsider the justiciability question, both Thomas and Scalia filed concurrences in which they reiterated their belief that political gerrymandering represents a nonjusticiable political question, and Justices Alito and Roberts each took no position on the issue, leaving open to debate how the two Bush appointees would vote if the question were to come before the court again. Nevertheless, the fact that Kennedy's majority opinion addresses the merits of the plaintiffs' claim of an unconstitutional partisan gerrymander would seem to imply justiciability, and in light of *LULAC,* the justiciability question appears to have been resolved for the time being.

Majority Opinion—Justice Kennedy

Justice Kennedy's constitutional reasoning rests on the assertion that the Texas plan must be upheld under standards put forward by the plaintiffs for determining whether a partisan gerrymander is unconstitutional, and so "because appellants have established no legally impermissible use of political classifications, they state no claim on which relief may be granted as to their contention that Texas' statewide redistricting is an unconstitutional political gerrymander" (548 U.S. 423). Article I, Section 4 of the Constitution gives "the States primary responsibility for apportionment of their . . . congressional . . . districts," while permitting Congress to impose additional standards; however, since "neither the Constitution nor Congress has stated any explicit prohibition of mid-decade redistricting to change districts drawn earlier in conformance with a decennial census," the constitutionality of such redistricting must be upheld (414). Kennedy rejects the notion that the sole purpose of the Texas redistricting was to increase partisan gain, noting that "some contested district lines seem to have been drawn based on more mundane and local interests, and a number of line-drawing requests by Democratic state legislators were honored," and citing the fact that the district court had found no evidence that the Republicans "intentionally sought to manipulate population variances" in enacting the plan (422).

The court also questioned whether partisan gerrymandering had actually taken place, given that the demonstrated effect of the Republican plan was largely just to bring the number of Republicans in Texas's congressional delegation more in line with the Republican percentage of the popular vote. While not reaching the effects test on the merits, given that the court did not find sufficient evidence of discriminatory intent to violate "one person, one vote," Justice Kennedy nevertheless concludes that "compared to the map challenged in *Vieth*, which led to a Republican majority in the congressional delegation despite a Democratic majority in the statewide vote, Plan 1374C can be seen as making the party balance more congruent to statewide party power" (419). As in *Vieth*, the justices appeared skeptical about the extent to which the challenged partisan gerrymandering plan actually created a significant electoral disadvantage for the party at which it was targeted.

This conclusion appears to be supported by the available electoral evidence, which casts significant doubt on the extent to which the challenged plan instituted electoral bias that was either severe or long-lasting. While the 2003 Texas redistricting offers one fewer election for analysis of the implications of the plan than was possible in Pennsylvania for the *Vieth* decision, when examining the results of the subsequent congressional elections in light of *LULAC*, a similar conclusion must be reached about the lack of discriminatory effect. At the time of the 1990 Census, the Democrats held nineteen of Texas's twenty-seven seats in the House, and also controlled both state legislative houses and the governorship, despite receiving only 51 percent of the statewide popular vote in the 1990 election. With Texas, like the rest of the South, becoming significantly more Republican, the Democrats implemented a redistricting plan that used extensive political gerrymandering in order to try and retain control. This plan itself had been challenged by Republicans as an unconstitutional political gerrymander in the wake of the court's decision in *Bandemer*; however, the suit was dismissed by a three-judge panel under the two-prong test. Table 3.1 shows the results of congressional elections in Texas following both the 1991 Democratic redistricting and the 2003 Republican redistricting.

The table illustrates that the Democrats were able to win twenty-one of Texas's thirty seats in 1992, and held on to a majority of the delegation throughout the 1990s despite losing control of both the governorship and the state senate. The question of why the Democrats were so successful at using gerrymandering to insulate their House majority in Texas when they failed so spectacularly in almost all other areas of the South, has been covered extensively in the political science literature. Black and Black (2002, 345) document a series of factors that prevented a Republican breakthrough in the state, including the Democrats' ability to take advantage of the three congressional seats gained as a result of reapportionment following the 1990 Census, their emphasis on protecting Democratic incumbents and marshaling the effects of the incumbency advantage in House elections to hold on to their existing seats, and their successful efforts to pack Republican voters into a few metropolitan/suburban districts, all of which voted at least

TABLE 3.1. Texas Congressional Election Results, 1992–2010

YEAR	SEATS WON IN CONGRESS		% OF TWO-PARTY VOTE		AVERAGE % MARGIN OF VICTORY	
	DEM	REP	DEM	REP	DEM	REP
1992	21	9	51.1	48.9	35.7	56.5
1994	19	11	43.0	57.0	22.2	63.9
1996	17	13	46.2	53.8	26.2	44.3
1998	17	13	46.1	53.9	49.5	58.6
2000	17	13	48.8	51.2	53.5	49.2
2002	17	15	45.1	54.9	47.1	54.9
2004	11	21	40.3	59.7	47.8	43.9
2006	13	19	45.7	54.3	57.3	32.3
2008	12	20	41.5	58.5	48.3	49.7
2010	9	23	32.1	67.9	30.4	55.4

SOURCE: U.S. House of Representatives, Office of the Clerk, "Election Statistics (1920–2010)," http://clerk.house.gov/members/electionInfo/elections.html (accessed July 3, 2012).

NOTES: Average % Margin of Victory = winning party's vote %–losing party's vote %, averaged across all districts won by that party. As a result of the Supreme Court's decision in *League of United Latin American Citizens v. Perry*, a number of districts were redrawn by the federal district court, and held open primaries on the day of the 2006 general election. In the Twenty-Third District, no candidate received an overall majority of the votes cast, and so a runoff election was held on December 12, 2006, to determine the winner. The vote totals from the runoff election and not the open primary are included in the analysis.

68 percent for George H. W. Bush in the 1988 presidential election, and where incumbent Republican House members continued to run up huge majorities throughout the 1990s. In other southern states, Democrats lacked the same advantages that allowed them to maintain their control of the Texas delegation, and their singular lack of success in using that control to effectively gerrymander led Grofman and Brunell (2005) to label these redistricting plans "dummymanders."

Despite their Texas success, in the face of a declining vote share, the 21–10 Democratic majority in the state's congressional delegation had eroded to just a 17–13 majority by 2000. The plan implemented by the district court and in place for the 2002 election left the 1991 Democratic gerrymander largely in place, and as a result, the Democrats retained a 17–15 majority in the Texas delegation despite a 55 percent to 45 percent deficit in the statewide popular vote. This was the situation at the time the new Republican redistricting plan was being drawn up in 2003, and so it is no surprise that the Republican Party was eager to redraw the Texas congressional map in a way that would reflect its growing partisan strength in the state.

In the first two congressional elections held under the Republican plan in 2004 and 2006, the Republicans won twenty-one and nineteen of Texas's thirty-two seats, respectively, while continuing to win a large majority of the statewide popular vote. In 2008, the Republicans won twenty of the thirty-two seats and retained a large majority in the statewide popular vote despite the improved Democratic performance in the nation as a whole on the coattails of a winning Democratic presidential candidate. In 2010, the collapse of the Democratic Party's electoral strength in the state continued, as they won just 32 percent of the statewide popular vote, and captured just nine of the thirty-two available seats. The "Margin of Victory" statistic in this case is even more telling than in Pennsylvania, with the Republicans winning significantly larger majorities in the districts they captured compared with the Democrats prior to 2004, a trend that was reversed in the two elections following the redistricting, and again in 2010. In 2008, the average margin of victory was approximately equal for both Democratic and Republican candidates. These results suggest that the 2003 Republican plan was in fact significantly fairer than the set of boundaries it replaced in terms of its effects on electoral competition. Though the 2003 mid-decade redistricting clearly favored the Republicans—a political science analysis of the five redistricting plans proposed by the legislature found that all five contained a significant partisan bias in favor of the Republican Party (McKee, Teigen, and Turgeon 2006)—it did not distort the results of subsequent elections to anything like the extent that the Democratic plan did in the 1990s.

Figure 3.1 plots the Democratic percentage of seats won and the Democratic share of the statewide two-party popular vote for each of the congressional elections in Texas from 1992 to 2010. It illustrates that the Democratic share of Texas's congressional seats tracks much more closely with their share of the statewide vote in the elections after the Republican gerrymander than it did in the elections before. The Democratic Party was able to win between 55 percent and 70 percent of the House seats in the state in each of the elections from 1992 to 2002, despite winning the statewide popular vote only once during that period, a narrow victory in 1992. The Democratic vote share declined to between 45 percent and 50 percent from 1994 to 2002, and then declined further to between 40 percent and 45 percent in the two subsequent elections. Most striking, the line for the Democratic seat percentage is much closer to the vote percentage line after the 2003 redistricting than it was before, as the Democrats won between 35 percent and 40 percent of the state's House seats in those elections. So, while the Republican Party clearly benefited from the redistricting plan—their share of the congressional delegation jumped almost 20 percentage points from 2002 to 2004, going from a 15–17 minority to a 21–11 majority—their improved performance is as much a result of increasing Republican vote share during this period as it is a product of redistricting. While the Democrats were able to rebound slightly in 2006, the aforementioned trend continues in 2008 and 2010, as

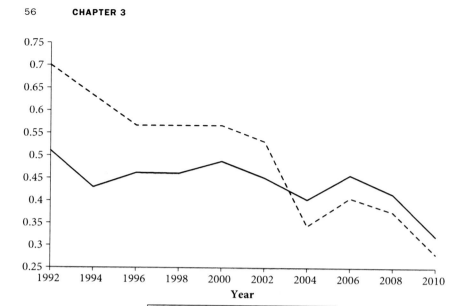

FIGURE 3.1. Democratic Seats and Votes in Texas, 1992–2010

both the Democratic share of the popular vote and their percentage of seats in the state congressional delegation continue to fall, and track even more closely with each other than they did from 2002 to 2004.

Figure 3.2 illustrates the seats-to-votes ratio for the Democratic and Republican parties in Texas from 1992 to 2010. It shows that, as was the case in Pennsylvania, the Democratic Party was, in fact, significantly overrepresented in Texas's congressional delegation throughout the 1990s, in particular during the early part of the decade immediately after the Democratic gerrymander was put into place. Nevertheless, as the Democratic vote percentage declined throughout the 1990s, their level of overrepresentation also declined, then remained static for the elections from 1996 to 2002. So, while the Democratic Party was still overrepresented in Texas at the time of the 2003 Republican gerrymander, the election results were not as disproportional as they had been in the wake of the 1990s gerrymander. The figure also illustrates that the level of disproportionality in the Texas delegation actually decreased following the passage of the 2003 plan and, indeed, the electoral system in the state appears to have treated both parties extremely fairly in the four subsequent elections.

Though the Republican Party was slightly overrepresented by 2010 given their share of the statewide vote, this imbalance is slightly smaller than that in favor

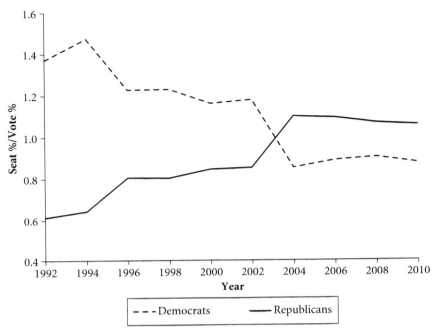

FIGURE 3.2.   Seats-to-Votes Ratio in Texas, 1992–2010

of the Democrats in the late 1990s, and significantly smaller than the electoral advantage enjoyed by the Democratic Party in 1992 and 1994. Far from distorting the results of subsequent elections, the alleged Republican gerrymander in Texas has actually moved the seats-to-votes ratio closer to proportionality in a way that reflects the growing Republican electoral strength in the state. As the *LULAC* case was pending before the Supreme Court, Senator John Cornyn of Texas defended the Republican plan, stating that "you can't take politics out of politics, and there is nothing more political than redistricting." He went on to note that "the history of electoral politics in Texas during the latter half of the twentieth century can be described as the story of the dominance, decline, and eventual eclipse of the Democratic Party as the state's majority party. It seems reasonable for the state's congressional delegation to reflect this reality" (quoted in Toobin 2006).

The empirical evidence would seem to directly contradict the conventional wisdom about the 2003 Republican redistricting, which is often hailed by commentators and journalists alike as the quintessential example of egregious partisan manipulation of district boundaries. But this line of analysis consistently turns on the partisan intent of the Republican plan rather than on an examination of its actual effects. There is no doubt that the intention of the Republican

Party in 2003 was to implement a configuration of districts that would increase their representation in the congressional delegation. There is ample evidence of this both in the legislative history of the plan itself and the lower courts record in *LULAC*, although the court did conclude that there was insufficient evidence to indicate that partisanship was the *sole* motivation behind the plan. But the Republicans' actions arguably only became necessary after the federal courts elected to implement a redistricting plan for the 2002 election that significantly diluted Republican voting strength. The results of elections following the alleged gerrymander have actually exhibited greater proportionality than those before it. As a majority of justices pointed out when the case reached the Supreme Court, there is nothing in the Constitution that prohibits mid-decade redistricting, even if it is conducted in the interest of securing partisan gains. Like Pennsylvania in *Vieth*, the evidence in Texas would appear to support the result the court reached in *LULAC*, though not necessarily the constitutional reasoning of Justice Kennedy, who maintains that partisan gerrymander may be unconstitutional based on a heretofore undiscovered "reliable measure of partisan fairness."

The Future of the Law

The state of the law on partisan gerrymandering in the wake of *LULAC* is therefore somewhat unclear. While the justiciability question appears to have been resolved for the time being, and while there appears to be a majority of the court that is willing to entertain the notion that some partisan gerrymanders might be unconstitutional, there exists no clear consensus on the issue. The court has yet to define what, if anything, it believes is unconstitutional about partisan gerrymandering, or to unite behind any one of the myriad standards that have been proposed for adjudicating such claims. Justice Kennedy's opinion in *LULAC* sets a precedent that even evidence that a redistricting plan was driven predominately by partisan concerns is insufficient to establish unconstitutional discriminatory intent. While the true implications of *LULAC* may be yet to emerge, an argument can be made that because of the divided nature of the court in the two recent decisions, the *Bandemer* precedent still stands as good law, and so lower courts should continue to apply the two-prong test when evaluating future claims of unconstitutional political gerrymandering.

A number of possible standards have been proposed for adjudicating political gerrymandering challenges that might form the basis of future jurisprudence on the issue. Perhaps the most interesting of these is the concept of "partisan symmetry" (King and Browning 1987), which was given significant consideration by the court in its *LULAC* opinion, after it was presented to them by a number of political scientists in an amicus brief (King et al. 2005). The court, while rejecting partisan symmetry as a standard for adjudicating political gerrymandering in the *LULAC* case, nevertheless expressed considerable encouragement for its potential use in the future as part of a broader test. Justice Stevens described it as "a helpful (though certainly not talismanic) tool" (548 U.S. 468); and Justices Souter and Ginsburg declined to "rule out the utility of a criterion of symmetry as a test," and concluded that "interest in exploring this notion is evident" (483); whereas Justice Kennedy also expressed some interest in the standard, although with the caveat that "asymmetry alone is not a reliable measure of unconstitutional partisanship" (420). Although decidedly lukewarm at this juncture, the court's comments on partisan symmetry represent "the first time for any proposal [that] the Court gave a clear indication that a future legal test for partisan gerrymandering will likely include partisan symmetry" (Grofman and King 2007). The main problem with the approach is that it would require the justices to set a particular threshold level of asymmetry at which a political gerrymander becomes unconstitutional, something they were unwilling to do in *LULAC*.

Another possibility for future litigation is to challenge political gerrymandering under other constitutional provisions besides the Fourteenth Amendment Equal Protection Clause and the First Amendment freedom of association, each of which has so far failed to produce a judicially manageable standard acceptable to a majority of the court. One approach might be to challenge the practice under the Elections Clause of Article I, Section 4 of the Constitution and the Qualifications Clause of Article I, Section 4, based on the precedents of *U.S. Term Limits Inc. v. Thornton* (514 U.S. 779 (1995)) and *Cook v. Gralike* (531 U.S. 510 (2001)). These cases held that the states' power to regulate the times, places, and manner of holding elections is limited to procedural regulations only, and cannot be used by states to attempt to dictate electoral outcomes In these cases, states had attempted to place additional qualifications on candidates for federal office by imposing either actual or de facto term limits (Greene 2005). Using this approach, partisan gerrymandering could be struck down as "an unconstitutional incursion into the sphere of power allocated to the national legislature and the national electorate" (Note 2004). The standard could be based on whether the gerrymander creates so many districts that are either uncontested or uncompetitive that the outcome of the election is effectively determined before the voters ever go to the polls.

Another possibility is for the court to extend the precedent of *Wesberry v. Sanders* to partisan gerrymandering, which could be held unconstitutional as an impermissible favoring by states of certain candidates over others, in violation of the requirement of Article I, Section 2 that representatives be elected "by the people." Each of these approaches hinges not on the discriminatory effect that political gerrymandering has on voters, but on the state governments' overstepping of their constitutional powers in implementing a gerrymander so severe that it effectively determines the outcome of subsequent elections. They also have the advantage of potentially offering judicially manageable standards that are much easier to define than those under the Equal Protection Clause, and that could be based on the number of challenged districts in which the election outcome is effectively predetermined. Although they may provide an effective blueprint for challenging partisan gerrymandering of congressional districts, neither of these can be extended to the states since Article I does not apply to the reapportionment of state legislatures. Both of these approaches would also require evidence linking control of redistricting directly to subsequent electoral disproportionality and lack of competition, neither of which was evident in either *Vieth* or *LULAC*.

In a related strand of litigation, opponents of partisan gerrymandering have also already achieved some significant successes by challenging states' redistricting plans in the state courts. This happened in *Salazar v. Davidson* (79 P.3d 1221 (Colo. 2003)), in which the plaintiffs successfully challenged Colorado's mid-decade redistricting on the basis that the state's constitution permitted only one decennial reapportionment, and *Wilkins v. West* (571 S.E. 2d 100 (Va. 2002)), which struck down Virginia's redistricting plan under the state constitution's requirements of contiguity and compactness. Given that state constitutions often contain significantly more provisions granting specific individual rights and governing the redistricting process in general, and since the Supreme Court has so far proven unwilling to hear appeals to state court decisions striking down political gerrymanders, this would appear to be the most prudent approach for opponents who might wish to challenge partisan gerrymandering in future litigation.

WINNING THE FUTURE?
REDISTRICTING AND PARTISAN BIAS

The Supreme Court's failure so far to agree on a coherent and definitive test with which to adjudicate the issue of partisan gerrymandering has been predicated in large part on the absence of evidence of pervasive and long-lasting effects sufficient to meet the *Davis v. Bandemer* standard. It is thus necessary to ascertain exactly how effective partisan gerrymandering has been in terms of its long-term benefits to the gerrymandering party. If the evidence reveals that partisan redistricting can significantly damage the opposition party's electoral fortunes for numerous subsequent electoral cycles, this may aid the court in determining a threshold for striking down its most egregious instances under the *Bandemer* precedent. However, if the effects of partisan gerrymandering are less severe and tend to fade over subsequent elections, then the court's widely criticized cautious approach and unwillingness to declare such plans unconstitutional may be vindicated.

In addition to shedding light on some of the questions confronted in redistricting litigation on the long-term electoral ramifications, these findings will also serve to answer an as yet undetermined question about the effectiveness of partisan redistricting as a policy and its allegedly damaging effects for democracy and electoral choice. Concrete evidence of the electoral effects of partisan redistricting may also help to provide a blueprint for the approach parties take when undertaking future rounds of redistricting. This analysis tests for the effects of control of redistricting on aggregate electoral disproportionality and partisan bias, as well as on the outcomes of elections in individual House districts.

Theoretical Perspectives

The first major implication of the constrained nature of the redistricting process for the effectiveness of partisan gerrymandering stems from uncertainly over the exact nature of the electorate and from tensions between the individual interests of incumbents and the collective interests of their party. Those in charge of drawing up redistricting plans have access to a great deal of information that may be helpful in crafting a partisan gerrymander, including data on the sociodemographic traits and political preferences of the electorate that are available at the individual precinct or city block level. Combined with the increasing sophistication of the computer software used for redistricting, this data allows specific districts to be individually tailored to serve partisan political interests (Monmonier 2001). However, knowledge of the current makeup and distribution of the electorate in the jurisdiction in question is still less than perfect. Redistricters may operate in a high-information environment, but they do not have access to complete information about individual voter preferences (Friedman and Holden 2008). Their knowledge of the existing political climate is offset by the significant degree of uncertainty that exists regarding future electoral outcomes, particularly with respect to the effects of turnout, voter displacement, generational replacement, and population mobility.

In the election immediately following redistricting, where the alignment of voters in a state most closely resembles that on which the redistricting plan was crafted, there is the potential for partisan gerrymandering of district boundaries to produce significant electoral effects. Redistricters can use knowledge of previous demographics, election results, and turnout patterns to quite accurately predict what is likely to happen in the next election and, with some degree of margin for error built in to account for uncertainty, implement a redistricting plan that effectively furthers partisan interests. Even this goal, however, may be thwarted by the effect that displacement of district populations can have in undermining the incumbency advantage, and the amount of uncertainty increases with each additional election following redistricting.

A number of factors can combine to dramatically alter the underlying distribution of voters that had formed the basis of a gerrymander. Generational replacement may alter a state's electorate considerably, especially in the presence of a secular realignment such as that which has been taking place in many areas of the South in recent decades (Abramowitz and Saunders 1998; Black and Black 2002). National electoral swings and turnout variations produced by coattail effects and patterns of surge and decline may alter the nature of the electoral environment at the state level, with the largest variation occurring between presidential elections and midterm years (Campbell 1986). Residential mobility through intra- and interstate migration may also substantially alter the geographical distribution of voters in a jurisdiction, especially since the effects of such demographic shifts over time are rarely politically neutral (Bishop 2008; Cho, Gimpel, and Hui 2013; McDonald 2011). All else being equal, the effectiveness of a partisan gerrymander is expected to decline as the alignment of voters moves further away from that on which the redistricting plan was based.

A second implication of this theory is that political parties are following a suboptimal strategy when they attempt to implement a political gerrymander that maximizes their vote efficiency. However, they are also necessarily limiting their potential short-term gains from redistricting when they attempt to safeguard the stability of those gains in the long run. The optimal approach for a party that has unilateral control over the redistricting process, and seeks to use that control to further partisan interests, is to maximize short-term gains while minimizing the potential for long-term losses. Put another way, the party desires to capture as many seats as possible in the election immediately following redistricting, but it also aims to hold on to that position of electoral strength and successfully defend those captured seats in future electoral cycles. The problem parties face is that, due to the inherent nature of the redistricting process, the short-term and long-term goals of partisan gerrymandering are directly at odds with one another. A party seeking to maximize its short-term gains from redistricting must necessarily do so by creating an efficient gerrymander that optimizes the party's vote efficiency. But keeping wasted votes to a minimum, and thus allowing the party to win the greatest number of seats possible given their strength in the popular vote, requires the creation of marginal seats. These seats, while likely increasing overall electoral competitiveness and responsiveness, work against the gerrymandering party in the long term since they are more difficult to defend in future elections than safe seats. Conversely, a party that desires to insulate itself against long-term electoral shocks must do so by making the seats it currently holds safer, but in so doing must also sacrifice vote efficiency and thus its chances of picking up additional seats from its opponents.

The major reason why the effects of redistricting are so transitory is that, given the choice between maximizing short-term partisan gains and securing the long-term stability of the party's existing electoral strength, parties tend to err toward the former rather than the latter. The pressures faced by redistricters are more evident at the state legislative level: party leaders in the state legislature are under pressure to use their control of the redistricting process to increase their party's seat allocation. Their positions in the party hierarchy also may be jeopardized by a less than impressive performance in the subsequent election. Similarly, those in control of redistricting face pressure from the national political parties to attempt to increase their seats in Congress, and congressional leaders, though not directly involved in the state-level process of redrawing district boundaries, may play an important informal role in crafting the various plans on offer. Politics, to be sure, is a results-oriented business, and with the popular perception being that redistricting effectively dictates the outcome of subsequent elections, party officials are under pressure to produce immediate results. According to Friedman and Holden (2008), the optimal partisan gerrymander, as opposed to the efficient gerrymander, involves the creation of the maximum number of safe seats that a party is able to secure through packing. In reality, parties in control of the redistricting process often tend to focus on the twin strategies of cracking and packing in an effort to increase the efficiency of their vote distribution in search of the effective gerrymander (Cox and Katz 2002).

The evidence suggests that in the presence of uncertainty about voter preferences and future electoral swings, political parties are frequently behaving suboptimally in the redistricting process. To be sure, there are examples of parties in unilateral control of the redistricting process implementing conservative political gerrymanders that focus more on protecting their incumbents than on making a concerted effort to add to their seat total. The Democratic redistricting plans in California following the 2000 Census and in Oklahoma after 1990 are examples of "safe" gerrymandering, as is the 2000 Republican plan in Kansas, but these are the exception rather than the norm. More frequently, self-interested politicians have incentives to maximize short-term electoral gains and, as a result, artificial majorities created through partisan redistricting are likely to be particularly susceptible to adverse popular vote swings in subsequent electoral cycles. While the marginal seats created by an efficient gerrymander may be lost in response to a relatively small swing toward the opposition party, the safer districts created through packing are much more likely to weather even the most significant of electoral storms.

Finally, the effectiveness of partisan gerrymandering is also likely to be conditional on changes in congressional apportionment. An increase in a state's allocation of congressional seats increases the pool of potential districts for the gerrymandering party to target, but it also increases the likelihood that a partisan gerrymander will be able to overcome the competing interests of incumbent self-protection. The added seat(s) provide flexibility to the gerrymandering party to protect its incumbent candidates while also creating competitive open seats that the party can capture. An increase in apportionment also allows the party to gerrymander more extensively than might be warranted by mere population change. Conversely, a decrease in a state's congressional seats creates significant problems for a party attempting to use the redistricting process for gerrymandering. Here, the interests of partisan advantage and incumbent protection are even more directly in competition with one other, as there are now fewer districts between which to allocate the existing incumbent members of

Congress, and less flexibility when it comes to the manipulation of district boundaries. A reduction in apportionment makes it almost impossible for a party to pick up seats while at the same time protecting its incumbents from being paired together or facing a strong challenge from the opposing party. Thus, the political pressures surrounding redistricting may negate the potential for effective gerrymandering of district boundaries under such circumstances.

Determining Control of Redistricting

The first step in testing the electoral implications of the various different types of redistricting is to determine, for each decennial redistricting cycle in each state, who was responsible for implementing the redistricting plan that ultimately determined the district boundaries for subsequent congressional elections. The approach taken to determine control of redistricting was to identify—through reference to and cross-referencing of multiple primary and secondary sources—which actors or combinations of actors were responsible for redistricting. The coding of particular redistricting plans as partisan, bipartisan, independent, or judicial was based on identifying the party in control of the redistricting process, rather than the intent of the individual congressional redistricting plan. So a state with unified partisan control at the time of redistricting was coded as partisan, regardless of whether the party chose to gerrymander extensively or not.

The goal of this approach was to isolate the direct effects of partisan control of the redistricting process from the incidental partisan consequences of redistricting in general. Coding redistricting based on control departs from the procedure employed in many previous studies, such as that by Gelman and King (1994), whose emphasis on retrospectively ascertaining the intent of each redistricting scheme risks endogenously conflating the observed partisan effects with the original aims of a plan. The procedure employed here is similar to that followed by Friedman and Holden (2009), with some minor modifications, most notably by taking into account the lack of a gubernatorial veto over redistricting plans in certain states and the inclusion of a separate category for independent commissions.

Coding was based on information obtained from the following sources: Congressional Quarterly's *Almanac of American Politics*, which contains detailed information on the redistricting process in each state for each redistricting cycle; the Voting and Democracy Research Center's state-by-state redistricting analyses, which include information on partisan control of state government and redistricting law at the state level; and the National Conference of State Legislatures Redistricting Task Force's database of redistricting litigation in both the state and federal courts. These sources yielded detailed information on the 1990 and 2000 redistricting cycles. Information on previous redistricting plans was both scarcer and less reliable, and so the focus in this chapter and in chapter 5 is on elections following the two most recent rounds of redistricting, for which there is a full decade of election results available. Based on the information obtained from the above sources, the following coding rules were developed in order to assign each state redistricting in the 1990s and 2000s cycles to one of four categories:

States Coded as Partisan

1. A single political party controls all three branches of state government. The redistricting plan is passed by the legislature and signed into law by the governor.
2. As 1, however, the plan is challenged in either the state or federal courts and is either substantially or entirely upheld.
3. A single political party controls both houses of the state legislature, but not the governorship. The redistricting plan is passed by the legislature and becomes law without the governor's signature.
4. A single political party controls both houses of the state legislature, but not the governorship. The redistricting plan is passed by the legislature over the governor's veto.

States Coded as Bipartisan

1. A single political party controls both houses of the state legislature, but not the governorship. The redistricting plan is passed by the legislature and signed into law by the governor.
2. One party controls the state house while another controls the state senate. The redistricting plan is passed by the legislature and signed into law by the governor.

States Coded as Independent

1. The state has turned over control of congressional redistricting to an independent commission, which draws up and approves the redistricting plan.
2. The political branches of the state government fail to pass a redistricting plan by the statutory or constitutional deadline. Under state law, a commission is impaneled to draw up and approve the redistricting plan.

States Coded as Judicial

1. The redistricting plan is challenged in the state or federal courts. The courts either substantially modify the plan or strike it down and impose an entirely new redistricting plan.

2. The political branches of the state government fail to pass a redistricting plan by the statutory or constitutional deadline. Under state law, the judiciary is empowered to draw up and approve the redistricting plan.

The unit of analysis for coding decisions was the state election cycle, thus taking into account situations where a state's congressional boundaries were redrawn multiple times within a single decade. In Texas, redistricting was coded as judicial for 2002, as the plan in place for that election was imposed by a special three-judge federal district court panel, and as partisan for the remainder of the decade, as a new plan was passed by the Republican state government prior to the 2004 election. The extensive redistricting litigation in the 1990s, which saw a number of states' congressional redistricting plans struck down by the federal courts in a series of racial gerrymandering cases, also necessitated multiple different codes for control of redistricting for different elections throughout that decade. The coding of each state redistricting for the 1990 and 2000 redistricting cycles is outlined in table 4.1, while table 4.2 summarizes the number of states in each category for both decades.

Seat Change following Congressional Redistricting

Does partisan control of the redistricting process subvert democracy by allowing that party to effectively dictate future election outcomes? Results from elections following the redistricting rounds of the 1990s and 2000s would certainly seem to demonstrate at least preliminary support for the theoretical expectations in the previous section, although the evidence from the raw seat change numbers is somewhat mixed. Table 4.3 displays the election results for each state delegation to the U.S. House of Representatives where there was unilateral partisan control of the redistricting process following the 2000 Census.

The data illustrate several interesting trends in the electoral fortunes of the political parties following a partisan-controlled redistricting. First and foremost, and not unexpectedly given the high-profile instances of partisan gerrymandering that have made the headlines in recent decades, the party that controlled the most recent round of redistricting was generally able to gain an immediate and significant boost in its number of seats in that state's congressional delegation. For the 2000s redistricting cycle, it appears that the Republican Party was able to gain greater short-term dividends from the eight states in which it controlled redistricting than the Democrats did in the nine states where they were in control,

TABLE 4.1. Control of Redistricting Classifications

STATE	1990s	2000s	STATE	1990s	2000s
Alabama	JUD	DEM	Montana	IND	IND
Alaska	BIP	IND	Nebraska	BIP	BIP
Arizona	JUD	IND	Nevada	DEM	BIP
Arkansas	DEM	DEM	New Hampshire	REP	BIP
California	JUD	DEM	New Jersey	IND	IND
Colorado	BIP	JUD	New Mexico	DEM	JUD
Connecticut	IND	IND	New York	BIP	BIP
Delaware	BIP	BIP	North Carolina	DEM	DEM
Florida	JUD	REP	North Dakota	BIP	REP
Georgia	DEM/JUD	DEM/REP	Ohio	BIP	REP
Hawaii	IND	IND	Oklahoma	DEM	JUD
Idaho	BIP	IND	Oregon	DEM	JUD
Illinois	JUD	BIP	Pennsylvania	BIP	REP
Indiana	BIP	IND	Rhode Island	DEM	BIP
Iowa	IND	IND	South Carolina	JUD/BIP	JUD
Kansas	JUD	REP	South Dakota	REP	REP
Kentucky	DEM	BIP	Tennessee	DEM	DEM
Louisiana	BIP/JUD	BIP	Texas	DEM	JUD/REP
Maine	BIP	BIP/JUD	Utah	REP	REP
Maryland	DEM	DEM	Vermont	BIP	BIP
Massachusetts	BIP	DEM	Virginia	DEM/BIP	REP
Michigan	JUD	REP	Washington	IND	IND
Minnesota	JUD	JUD	West Virginia	DEM	DEM
Mississippi	JUD	JUD	Wisconsin	BIP	BIP
Missouri	BIP	BIP	Wyoming	BIP	REP

SOURCES: Congressional Quarterly (1998; 2008), National Conference of State Legislatures (2008; 2011).
NOTES: DEM = Democratic Party controlled redistricting.
REP = Republican Party controlled redistricting.
BIP = Redistricting was bipartisan.
IND = An independent commission controlled redistricting.
JUD = Redistricting was controlled by the federal or state courts.

TABLE 4.2. Control of Redistricting by Decade

	NUMBER OF STATES	
	1990s	2000s
Democratic Gerrymander	14	9
Republican Gerrymander	4	10
Bipartisan Redistricting	16	13
Independent Commission	6	10
Judicial Redistricting	10	8

NOTES: Numbers correspond to the first redistricting following each census. Excludes mid-decade redistricting.

TABLE 4.3. Seat Change in U.S. House Delegations after Redistricting, 2000–2010

	2000		2002		2004		2006		2008		2010		TOTAL	
	D	R	D	R	D	R	D	R	D	R	D	R	D	R
Democrats Controlled Redistricting:														
Alabama	2	5							**+1**	*−1*	*−2*	**+2**	*−1*	**+1**
Arkansas	3	1									*−2*	**+2**	*−2*	**+2**
California	32	20	**+1**				**+1**	*−1*					**+2**	*−1*
Georgia[1]	3	8	**+2**		**+1**	*−1*					*−1*	**+1**	**+2**	0
Maryland	4	4	**+2**	*−2*					**+1**	*−1*	*−1*	**+1**	**+2**	*−2*
Mass.	10	0											0	0
N. Carolina	5	7	**+1**				**+1**	*−1*	**+1**	*−1*	*−1*	**+1**	**+2**	*−1*
Tennessee	4	5	**+1**	*−1*							*−3*	**+3**	*−2*	**+2**
W. Virginia	2	1									*−1*	**+1**	*−1*	**+1**
Total			**+7**	*−3*	**+1**	*−1*	**+2**	*−2*	**+3**	*−3*	*−11*	**+11**	**+2**	**+2**
Republicans Controlled Redistricting:														
Florida	8	15	*−1*	**+3**			**+2**	*−2*	**+1**	*−1*	*−4*	**+4**	*−2*	**+4**
Kansas	1	3					**+1**	*−1*	*−1*	**+1**	*−1*	**+1**	*−1*	**+1**
Michigan	9	7	*−3*	**+2**					**+2**	*−2*	*−2*	**+2**	*−3*	**+2**
Ohio	8	11	*−2*	**+1**			**+1**	*−1*	**+3**	*−3*	*−5*	**+5**	*−3*	**+2**
Pennsylvania	10	11	*−3*	**+1**			**+4**	*−4*	**+1**	*−1*	*−5*	**+5**	*−3*	**+1**
Texas[2]	17	13		**+2**	*−6*	**+6**	**+2**	*−2*	*−1*	**+1**	*−3*	**+3**	*−8*	**+10**
Utah	1	2											0	0
Virginia	4	6	*−1*	**+2**					**+3**	*−3*	*−3*	**+3**	*−1*	**+2**
Total			*−10*	**+11**	*−6*	**+6**	**+10**	*−10*	**+8**	*−8*	*−23*	**+23**	*−21*	**+22**

SOURCE: Congressional Quarterly (2008).

NOTES: Includes states where one party was able to exert unilateral control over redistricting without unified control of state government (Arkansas, Massachusetts, Tennessee). Bold figures represent a net gain of seats, whereas italicized figures represent a net loss.

[1] District boundaries in Georgia were redrawn a second time by the Republican Party in 2005.

[2] Republican redistricting in Texas did not occur until 2003. The district boundaries in place for the 2002 election were drawn up by a special three-judge federal district court panel.

with the Republicans picking up eleven seats and the Democrats seven in the 2002 midterm election. Following the 2003 Texas redistricting, the Republicans were able to pick up an additional six congressional seats in the 2004 election, while the Democrats gained one additional seat, bringing their total seats gained to seventeen and eight, respectively, including seats that were added to these various states as a result of reapportionment. The Republican Party's initial gains from partisan gerrymandering are therefore at least partly responsible for the party's impressive performance in the 2002 midterm election, where it bucked the trend of a president's party almost always losing seats in the House of Representatives

(Campbell 1987). These results are consistent with the idea that the electoral effects of partisan gerrymandering are likely to be strongest in the election immediately following redistricting.

What the data also illustrate is the susceptibility of electoral majorities obtained through redistricting to subsequent adverse swings in the national popular vote. Of the thirty-one seats gained by the Democrats in taking back control of the House of Representatives in the 2006 midterm election, ten came from states in which the Republicans had controlled redistricting after 2000, and just two from the states where the Democrats had controlled the redistricting process. In 2008, the Democrats picked up an additional eight seats in Republican states, while losing control of two, and captured just three seats in Democratic states. After gaining seventeen seats from the Democrats in states where they controlled redistricting in 2000, by the end of the 2008 election cycle, the Republicans were actually worse off in those states than they had been prior to redistricting, losing eighteen seats to the Democrats in subsequent elections. These results are consistent with the notion that the electoral advantage gained by the party controlling redistricting would be likely to decline in subsequent electoral cycles.

Of course, these seats can always be won back when the national electoral tide turns in favor of the party implementing the gerrymander, as occurred in the Republican landslide during the 2010 midterm. In the 2010 election, the Republican Party not only recaptured the eighteen seats lost to the Democrats in 2006 and 2008, but also won another five seats in the states where they had controlled redistricting following the 2000 census. With the eight-point popular vote swing from 2008 to 2010, the Republicans therefore actually found themselves in an even better position in these states than they had been immediately following redistricting in 2002 or 2004. Yet many of the Republican gains in 2010 also came from states in which the Democrats had controlled redistricting after 2000, where they were able to reverse the steady uptick in Democratic strength that had been occurring since 2002. The 2010 landslide also included a Republican pickup of eleven seats in Democratic states in addition to the twenty-three seats from Republican states, for a total of thirty-four seats gained in states where partisan gerrymandering had occurred earlier in the decade.

Figure 4.1 illustrates this trend graphically, displaying the number of seats gained over their 2000 baseline by the parties that controlled the redistricting process. Though the figure does demonstrate the redistricting bump for the controlling party in the election immediately after the redrawing of congressional boundaries, followed by a steady decline in their electoral strength in

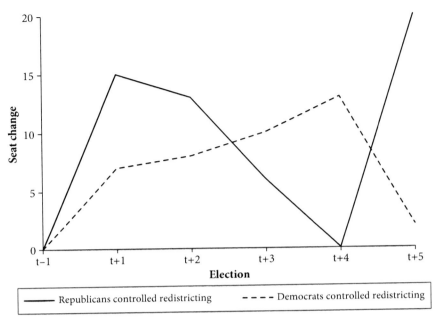

FIGURE 4.1. Control of Redistricting and Subsequent Electoral Strength, 2000–2010

NOTES: Totals represent seat changes in states with partisan redistricting at time (t), relative to the baseline of the 2000 election (t − 1). In Texas, the baseline is 2002.

each subsequent election, perhaps the most striking feature is the dramatically divergent trends for the two major political parties. Though the Democrats gained far less of a short-term advantage in the states where they controlled the redistricting process, they continued to steadily increase their seat totals in those states with their growing electoral strength in the latter part of the decade. In contrast, the Republicans, who received a far larger bump in their seat totals in states where they were in control of redistricting, have experienced a precipitous decline in their electoral strength in subsequent congressional elections. This trend is consistent with the idea that the electoral advantage gained by the gerrymandering party would decline most significantly in response to an adverse electoral swing against that party. In the 2000s redistricting cycle, the Republican gains from redistricting were observed to decline precipitously once there was a swing in the popular vote toward the Democrats in 2006 and 2008.

In 2010, the sheer magnitude of the Republican landslide is apparent in the dramatic changes illustrated by both lines on the graph. Not only did the party regain all the seats it had lost to the Democrats in Republican states in 2006 and 2008, plus several more, they also nearly wiped out the Democratic gains from redistricting in Democratic states that had manifested over the course of the decade. Given the dramatic nature of the swing in both seats and votes in the 2010 midterm, however, which represented the greatest loss of seats by a party in a House midterm election since the seventy-two that Franklin D. Roosevelt's Democrats surrendered to the Republicans in 1938, we should perhaps be cautious about reading too much into these results.

The data from the 2000s redistricting cycle also reveal some support for the importance of reapportionment to the efficacy of partisan gerrymandering. It appears that redistricters are considerably constrained from pursuing partisan goals in states that have lost seats in Congress, whereas partisan manipulation almost guarantees that those controlling the redistricting process will be able to take control of any congressional seats a state gains as a result of reapportionment. Of the twenty-four congressional districts the party controlling redistricting was able to capture in the subsequent election, seven were in states that gained representation in Congress as a result of reapportionment, whereas just four were in states that had lost seats in Congress.

Though a very different pattern emerges in the data from the 1990s redistricting cycle in table 4.4, similar dynamics are arguably at work. The most interesting finding is the sheer number of states in which the Democratic Party controlled redistricting after 1990, of which there are fourteen, whereas the Republican Party only had unilateral control of redistricting in two very small states, thus significantly blunting any potential electoral gains. What the data reveal, as illustrated in figure 4.2, is a complete inability on the part of the Democrats to insulate their electoral strength against subsequent adverse electoral shocks in states where they controlled redistricting. Not only were these states already trending in the direction of the Republican Party by this time—most notably, the nine southern and border states included in the Democratic column—but the dramatic swing in the national popular vote in the 1994 midterm saw the Democrats lose a significant number of seats in the states where they had controlled the redistricting process. Of the fifty-four seats the Republicans gained in 1994, twenty-one were from the fourteen states in which the Democrats had controlled redistricting after the 1990 Census, and nineteen of these were in southern and border states—a remarkably high proportion.

The evidence from the 1990s does not show the immediate boost in the electoral fortunes of the party controlling redistricting in 1992 that we observed in 2002, although we do see a precipitous decline in its seat totals in subsequent elections, an effect that can be mostly attributed to the Republican landslide of 1994. This indicates that not only were they unable to use control of redistricting

TABLE 4.4. Seat Change in U.S. House Delegations after Redistricting, 1990–2000

	1990		1992		1994		1996		1998		2000		TOTAL	
	D	R	D	R	D	R	D	R	D	R	D	R	D	R
Democrats Controlled Redistricting:														
Arkansas	3	1	-1	+1							+1	-1	0	0
Georgia[1]	9	1	-2	+3	-4	+4							-6	+7
Kentucky	4	3		-1	-2	+2	-1	+1					-3	+2
Maryland	5	3	-1	+1									-1	+1
Nevada	1	1			-1	+1			+1	-1			0	0
New Mexico	1	2					-1	+1	+1	-1			0	0
N. Carolina[2]	7	4	+1		-4	+4	+2	-2	-1	+1			-2	+3
Oklahoma	4	2			-3	+3	-1	+1			+1	-1	-3	+3
Oregon	4	1			-1	+1	+1	-1					0	0
Rhode Island	1	1			+1	-1							+1	-1
Tennessee	6	3			-2	+2							-2	+2
Texas	19	8	+2	+1	-3	+3	-1	+1					-2	+5
Virginia[3]	6	4	+1		-1	+1					-1	+1	-1	+2
W. Virginia	4	0	-1								-1	+1	-2	+1
Total			-1	+5	-20	+20	-1	+1	+1	-1	0	0	-21	+25
Republicans Controlled Redistricting:														
New Hampshire	1	1			-1	+1							-1	+1
Utah	2	1			-1	+1	-1	+1			+1	-1	-1	+1
Total			0	0	-2	+2	-1	+1	0	0	+1	-1	-2	+2

SOURCE: Congressional Quarterly (1998).

NOTES: Bold figures represent a net gain of seats, whereas italicized figures represent a net loss.

[1] Georgia's congressional districts were redrawn by a special three-judge federal district court panel following the Supreme Court's ruling in *Miller v. Johnson* (1995).

[2] North Carolina's Democratic redistricting plan remained largely in effect with only minor modifications through the 1996 election, after which a more extensive redrawing was undertaken following the Supreme Court's ruling in *Shaw v. Hunt* (1996).

[3] Virginia's Democratic redistricting plan was modified only slightly prior to the 1994 and 1996 elections, but the boundaries were redrawn extensively for the 1998 election following the federal district court's ruling in *Moon v. Meadows* (1997).

to increase their seat total, but that they were also unable to gerrymander in a way that preserved the seats that they were otherwise in danger of losing in 1994. Based on the evidence from the 1990s redistricting cycle, it seems likely that any potential advantage to the Democratic Party from redistricting was immediately blunted by the precipitous decline in its electoral fortunes in the South during that decade. Of the fourteen states in which the Democrats controlled redistricting, nine were southern or border states that were almost universally, with the

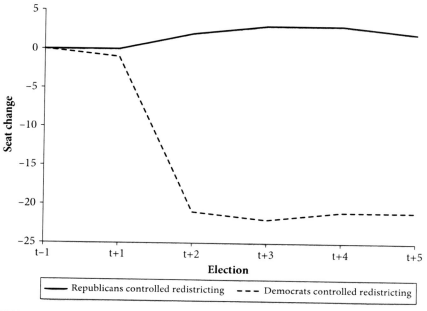

FIGURE 4.2. Control of Redistricting and Subsequent Electoral Strength, 1990–2000

Note: Totals represent seat changes in states with partisan redistricting at time (t), relative to the baseline of the 1990 election (t–1).

exception of Maryland, trending Republican at the time. This severely mitigated any possibility of making significant electoral gains through gerrymandering. Not only were Democratic line drawers in these states constrained by the pressure they received from the Department of Justice to create as many majority-minority districts as possible, forcing them to pack large numbers of overwhelmingly Democratic minority voters into a few supermajority districts (Black and Black 2002), but they also faced the acceleration of a secular realignment of southern whites in favor of the Republican Party that had been under way since the 1970s. The result was that many of the white voters who had been redrawn into new districts ended up supporting Republican House candidates in elections during the 1990s (McKee 2008; Petrocik and Desposato 1998). Only in Texas, where the Democrats faced a much more favorable climate due to the influences of incumbency, population patterns, and the creation of new seats due to reapportionment, was redistricting able to protect them against the rising Republican tide (Black and Black 2002).

In most cases, therefore, the partisan advantage gained from gerrymandering appears to be extremely transitory, with those seats captured through redistricting more likely to switch back to the original party of control in the face of adverse electoral conditions. This is particularly true when underlying electoral conditions in the state are essentially competitive, as has been the case in Pennsylvania since the redistricting there in the 2000s. Redistricting does not insulate a party's electoral majority in the face of popular sentiment, and the more seats a party attempts to gain through gerrymandering, the more seats it is likely to lose in subsequent elections if the popular vote shifts in the opposite direction. Similarly, when a party controls redistricting in a state in which its electoral strength is declining, it is unlikely to be able to use partisan gerrymandering to preserve the existing seat distribution in the face of a declining popular vote share, as happened with the Democrats in the South during the 1990s. It is only the combination of both partisan gerrymandering and a state that is realigning in favor of the party implementing the gerrymander that seems to be effective in fostering a long-term electoral advantage, as has been the case in Texas since the 2003 mid-decade redistricting. While these data do not demonstrate a causal relationship between redistricting and seat change in Congress, they are indicative of the general trends in congressional elections in states where a single political party had unilateral control of the redistricting process, and cast considerable doubt on the utility of partisan gerrymandering as a mechanism for instituting long-term electoral bias.

Data and Methods

In order to test for the effects of partisan gerrymandering in the 2000s redistricting cycle, data on congressional elections results at both the state delegation level and the district level were collected for the 2002–2010 elections. For the 1990s redistricting cycle, comparable data were collected for the elections from 1990 to 2000. The unit of analysis at the aggregate level was the state delegation to the House of Representatives, while the unit of analysis at the district level was the individual congressional seat. Since no redistricting can occur there, states with just a single at-large U.S. House district were excluded from both the district- and aggregate-level analyses. The excluded states were Alaska, Delaware, Montana, North Dakota, South Dakota, Vermont, and Wyoming. Across the two levels of analysis, three different operationalizations of the dependent variable were utilized in order to examine the causal link between control of redistricting and subsequent election results: two at the state delegation level, and one at the district level.

Dependent Variables

The appropriate measure of electoral disproportionality or bias very much depends on the level of analysis at which it is being assessed. For a legislature as a whole, or a subset thereof, bias is most often captured using some variation of the "partisan symmetry" standard, which measures the extent to which an electoral system treats parties differently in the way it translates vote percentages into legislative seats (King and Browning 1987). There have been two different approaches to measuring aggregate bias in a legislature: one based on the mean district vote percentage for a given election (Campagna and Grofman 1990; King and Gelman 1991), and the other based on the aggregate vote percentage for the legislature as a whole (Campbell 1996; Tufte 1973). This choice of operationalization has significant implications for conclusions about partisan bias and the importance of redistricting. Studies using the mean district vote percentage to calculate bias have often found a significant pro-Republican bias in U.S. House elections, and attribute a large portion of that bias to partisan gerrymandering (Gelman and King 1994; Grofman and King 2007).

However, studies using the total congressional vote have found a significant bias in favor of the Democratic Party in House elections, and as Campbell (1996, 129) notes, very little of this bias can be attributed to the effects of redistricting. Jacobson (1990), in a two-part analysis, estimates partisan bias in House elections from 1946 to 1988 using both of these alternative measures. The first part of his analysis, using the national congressional vote, finds a 2 percent pro-Democratic bias from 1946 to 1964 and a 4 percent pro-Democratic bias from 1966 to 1988, whereas the second part, using the average district vote, finds a large pro-Republican bias in the first period and a negligible pro-Republican bias in the second period. Here, both approaches were utilized.

First, at the state congressional delegation level (i), electoral disproportionality was operationalized as the difference between a party's share of the vote statewide ($V\%$) and its share of congressional seats won ($S\%$) within the state's delegation (Cox and Katz 2002), a measure known as the deviation from proportionality (DFP). Though similar to the concept of bias, disproportionality and partisan bias are not synonymous with one another. This is because an electoral system need not allocate seats proportionally to votes to be considered "unbiased," and so it becomes essential when using disproportionality as a measure of electoral fairness to control for the other potential sources of disproportionality. Following an approach similar to that used by Campbell (1996) to operationalize electoral bias in the House of Representatives as a whole, the total aggregate congressional vote for a state was used to calculate state-level disproportionality rather than the mean district vote. By using the following formula, we can calculate the deviation from proportionality for each state election:

$$DFP_i = S\%_i - V\%_i$$

This measure captures the extent to which a party is overrepresented (indicated by a positive value) or underrepresented (indicated by a negative value) in terms of its number of seats in Congress given its statewide share of the popular vote, compared to a system that allocates seats proportionately to electoral strength. In the first set of empirical models, the dependent variable is the Democratic deviation from proportionality (partisan electoral disproportionality). Since this measure is based on two-party vote and seat percentages for U.S. House elections, Republican DFP within a state delegation is simply the inverse of Democratic DFP. Positive values of partisan electoral disproportionality therefore indicate a bias toward the Democratic Party, whereas negative values indicate a bias toward the Republican Party.

Second, bias can also be measured at the aggregate level using the mean district vote and the partisan symmetry standard mentioned previously. The measurement of this dependent variable followed a similar approach to that used by Gelman and King (1994, 545) in their seminal study of the effects of redistricting on state legislative elections. They operationalize bias as "the deviation from partisan symmetry when the average district vote is between $v = .45$ and $v = .55$," so in an unbiased system, if the Democrats receive 75 percent of the seats from winning 55 percent of the popular vote, then the Republicans should also win 75 percent of the seats if they were to receive the same proportion of the popular vote. Bias is therefore defined as "the proportion of seats in the legislature that the Democrats receive over and above what is fair according to this symmetry criterion" (545).

While bias is usually measured in a legislature as a whole, a similar approach can be utilized to estimate the level of partisan bias in states grouped by the type of redistricting that has occurred, as well as in certain individual state house delegations. Using the JudgeIt II software developed by Gelman, King, and Thomas (2012), partisan bias can be estimated for states in which redistricting was partisan, either Democratic or Republican; states in which redistricting was bipartisan; and states in which redistricting was independent. In this way, overall levels of partisan bias in these different categories of states can be compared for both the 1990s and 2000s redistricting cycles. In addition, a measure comparable to the electoral disproportionality standard mentioned above can be obtained by calculating the partisan bias for each state delegation year, providing an alternative operationalization for statistical analysis of the effects of redistricting on subsequent elections. JudgeIt works by constructing a model of a two-party electoral system over multiple electoral cycles, then using that model to simulate quantities of interest such as partisan bias and electoral responsiveness.

The JudgeIt software was used to model the outcomes of house elections as a function of incumbency, the normalized district presidential vote, and campaign spending. Utilizing the partisan symmetry standard, JudgeIt then simulates the outcome of these elections under certain hypothetical conditions and compares the real results to the counterfactual of an electoral system that is unbiased, that is, it favors neither party in the translation of the statewide vote share into the partisan division of legislative seats. In the second set of empirical models, the dependent variable was this measure of partisan bias calculated using JudgeIt, with positive values once again indicating a pro-Democratic bias, and negative values indicating a pro-Republican bias.

At the individual district level, the effects of redistricting on election results can best be captured using a dichotomous measure of whether the Democratic candidate won or lost a particular election. Though many studies of congressional elections use a continuous measure of the Democratic share of the two-party popular vote, this measure is not appropriate for gauging the effects of redistricting. The goal of gerrymandering is not to maximize vote share, but instead to maximize the efficiency of those votes by capturing the maximum possible share of the available seats. An effective gerrymander will allow a party to win a greater number of seats given the same overall share of the popular vote. If gerrymandering is effective, therefore, we would expect to see a positive effect on the probability of winning individual seats in states where a party controlled redistricting, compared with states where it did not. This use of a dichotomous measure of congressional election outcomes when assessing the effects of redistricting is the same approach used by Friedman and Holden (2009) in their study of the effects of redistricting on rising incumbent reelection rates.

Independent Variables

The major independent variable of interest at each level of analysis is the presence or absence of a partisan gerrymander in the two most recent redistricting cycles. The states where one political party controlled redistricting were coded as 1, and all other states were coded as 0. Control of redistricting was also operationalized as a series of dummy variables, each coded as 1 if redistricting was controlled by the Democratic Party or the Republican Party, was implemented by an independent commission, or was conducted by the judiciary. The omitted category was therefore bipartisan redistricting. This allows for estimation and comparison of the different partisan effects of various types of redistricting.

Some studies of gerrymandering have classified redistricting based not on partisan control of the process but on the actual outcome of the redistricting itself. So, rather than identifying the party that exerted control over the actual drawing of lines—be it the legislature, the courts, or an independent commission—these studies classify redistricting as partisan based on whether the actual plan itself seemed to favor a particular party over the other. Under this standard, the 2000s redistricting in California would be coded as bipartisan even though the Democrats controlled the process, since the final plan largely preserved existing electoral alignments and protected incumbents. In contrast, the Texas redistricting plan that was put in place for the 2002 election, though drawn by the courts rather than the legislature, would be coded as partisan Democratic since it largely left in place the 1990s Democratic gerrymander. These outcome-based rather than control-based measures of redistricting are, as Friedman and Holden (2009, 598) point out, not only endogenous to the process itself but also potentially tainted by hindsight once the results of subsequent elections are actually observed. Control-based measures have the advantage of being completely objective, exogenous to the subsequent political negotiations and infighting that often characterize the redistricting process, and untainted by post hoc contamination from the actual election results once a plan has gone into effect.

Also following the approach of Friedman and Holden (2009), this chapter adopts a regression discontinuity approach in order to separate smooth changes in partisan bias over time from discrete jumps caused by the sudden reconfiguration of district boundaries. This approach necessitates the incorporation of two additional control variables in the analysis in addition to the measures of partisan gerrymandering, as well as some alterations to the model specifications, which are discussed below. First, a continuous time trend was included in order to control for other important factors unrelated to gerrymandering that may have changed smoothly over time. Second, a discrete step function was also included, with jumps that capture the overall effects of each complete redistricting cycle. So, a dummy variable was included for the 1990s redistricting, which was coded as 0 for the 1990 election and 1 for every subsequent election, and a second dummy variable was included for the 2000s redistricting, likewise set at 0 for every election prior to 2002 and at 1 thereafter (1990 serves as the baseline year). The overall effect of these controls is to allow us to isolate the effects of partisan gerrymandering from both long-term and short-term confounders stemming from the effects of redistricting overall, and other important omitted variables that may have changed over time.

There is also significant reason to believe that the levels of electoral disproportionality at the aggregate level should be affected by other factors besides redistricting. Therefore, several additional control variables were included in the analysis.

Research has demonstrated that the relationship between a party's seat percentage and vote percentage in a single-member plurality electoral system can be nonlinear (Tufte 1973). Specifically, such systems contain a significant "winner's bonus," whereby the party that wins the popular vote picks up more seats than they would under a system based on proportional representation (Grofman 1982). The electoral disproportionality measure picks up both this responsiveness of the electoral system to changes in voter preferences, as well as any potential unfairness in the translation of votes into seats. In order to control for the responsiveness component of the measure, and thus isolate the extent to which the electoral system in a state is biased toward one political party or the other, the aggregate models included a measure of the margin of victory in the statewide popular vote for that election. This was used to control for the winner's bonus, and was measured as the Democratic vote percentage minus the Republican vote percentage. This variable could also be measured using the log of the margin of victory, in order to take into account the nonlinear nature of the winner's bonus. Doing so produced no significant changes in the results.

There are also several reasons to expect election results to be influenced by changes in congressional apportionment. A party may pick up seats in a state that has gained representation, while the same change in the popular vote may not yield an equivalent increase in seats if a state has lost representation. For this reason, the models included a control variable measuring whether or not a state gained representation in the House as a result of the previous reapportionment, either 1990 or 2000. To control for the influence of the size of a state's House delegation, whereby the seats-to-votes ratio is likely to change more significantly and create greater disproportionality in small states than in large ones, a dummy variable was included for states with five or fewer congressional seats. Utilizing continuous measures of apportionment change and delegation size introduced significant multicollinearity into the models, and so the dichotomous measures were preferred. Conclusions regarding the effects of control of redistricting were unchanged by these coding decisions.

The electoral disproportionality models also included a number of additional controls to account for other sources of electoral disproportionality. Potential coattail effects were controlled for by the inclusion of dummy variables for the presence of a winning Democratic presidential, senatorial, or gubernatorial candidate in each state for each election, although coding coattail effects as the margin of victory in the up-ticket races produced no significant changes in the results. To account for the possible impact that districts where one of the major parties failed to field a candidate might have on the seats-to-votes ratio, a control variable was included for uncontested districts. This was measured as the number of uncontested Democratic districts minus the number of uncontested

Republican districts for each state electoral cycle. An alternate approach to this problem would be to adjust the House vote to account for uncontested districts along the lines of Jacobson (1993). Doing so produced no substantive changes in the results or conclusions.

At the district level, several control variables were included that, in addition to the influence of redistricting, were expected to affect the probability of the Democratic candidate winning the election. First, the effects of money were controlled for by including a measure of the candidates' campaign expenditures. This was operationalized not as it is in many studies, as the absolute dollar amount or the log of expenditures, but as the ratio of Democratic to Republican candidates' spending following the approach by Gierzynski and Breaux (1993) and Seabrook (2010). This measure makes greater theoretical sense than the inclusion of Democratic and Republican candidates' expenditures separately, as spending is only expected to affect the outcome of the election to the extent that one candidate is outspending the other, and by what amount. The spending ratio (SR) was calculated using the following formula:

$$SR = \frac{(\text{Democratic Expenditures} - \text{Republican Expenditures})}{(\text{Democratic Expenditures} + \text{Republican Expenditures})}$$

The resulting measure ranges from a value of -1, representing a situation where all the money in a particular district is spent by the Republican candidate, to a value of 1, representing a situation where all the money in a district is spent by the Democratic candidate. The midpoint of 0 represents a district where the Democratic and Republican candidates spend equal amounts of money.

Campaign expenditures should only have an impact in a particular race if they affect a candidate's electoral prospects above and beyond the predictive power of the district's partisan baseline. For this reason, Democratic Party strength was also controlled for in the district level analysis. Though ideally this would be operationalized as the percentage of registered or eligible voters who identify with the Democratic Party, this data is not available at the individual congressional district level. Instead, as had been done in many previous studies of congressional election results, party strength was operationalized using an indirect measure derived from the district presidential vote. In order to account for the fact that the district presidential vote may rise and fall with the results of each presidential election, this variable was measured as the deviation of the district presidential vote from the national presidential vote. This variable therefore takes on positive values where the Democratic presidential vote share in a district is larger than the Democratic presidential vote share at the national level, and negative values where it is smaller. For midterm congressional elections, the results of the preceding presidential election were used. As an additional control, the lagged Democratic vote share in the district from the previous congressional election was also included, as was a measure of incumbency coded as 1 where there was a Democratic inclement running for reelection, −1 where there was a Republican incumbent, and 0 where there was an open seat.

Redistricting and Partisan Electoral Disproportionality

Table 4.5 presents the results of the first set of empirical analyses of the effects of partisan gerrymandering on subsequent election results. The aforementioned measure of partisan electoral disproportionality was the dependent variable, and the level of analysis was the individual state house delegation. The results for multiple redistricting cycles were combined into a single statistical model, following the approach used by Friedman and Holden (2009). Also following their approach, the models in table 4.5 were estimated with state fixed effects, a time trend to control for any changes that may have taken place over the period under analysis, and dummy variables for the 1990s and 2000s redistricting cycles to capture the decadal shifts that occur after each redistricting takes place. The models were estimated using ordinary least squares (OLS) regression, with robust standard errors clustered by state. Combining data from all U.S. House elections that took place from 1990 to 2010 yielded 473 cases for analysis, once at-large states were excluded. Model 1 is the baseline model, incorporating each of the aforementioned controls for other possible sources of electoral disproportionality, while models 2 and 3 address the impact of partisan control of the redistricting process. Model 2 uses an overall measure of partisan gerrymandering, coded as 1 for states where the Democrats controlled redistricting, −1 for states where the Republicans controlled redistricting, and 0 for all other states. Model 3 incorporates separate dummy variables for Democratic states and Republican states, with all other states serving as the excluded category. Since redistricting conducted by either the courts or by an independent commission are not expected to produce partisan effects, they were not considered as separate categories at this stage of the analysis.

Turning first to the baseline model (model 1), the coefficients for the 1990s and 2000s redistricting cycles reveal that the Democratic Party experienced significant negative electoral effects from the 1990s redistricting taken as a whole. This is in keeping with much of the earlier discussion, and probably reflects the secular realignment occurring in the South during this period. In contrast, the coefficient for the 2000s cycle is positive and comes close to statis-

TABLE 4.5. Gerrymandering and Partisan Electoral Disproportionality in U.S. House Elections, 1990–2010

	(1)	(2)	(3)
Time Trend	−.002 (.002)	−.002 (.002)	−.002 (.002)
1990s Redistricting	−.066** (.022)	−.077** (.023)	−.061* (.023)
2000s Redistricting	.042 (.024)	.048* (.023)	.054* (.023)
Partisan Gerrymander	—	−.038 (.019)	—
Democratic Gerrymander	—	—	−.003 (.017)
Republican Gerrymander	—	—	−.097* (.036)
Apportionment	.013 (.034)	.009 (.028)	.001 (.026)
Small State	−.003 (.026)	.005 (.034)	−.019 (.025)
Uncontested Districts	−.015 (.009)	−.015 (.009)	−.014 (.009)
Senatorial Candidate	.010 (.011)	.012 .011	(.011) (.008)
Presidential Candidate	−.003 (.008)	−.003 (.008)	−.001 (.008)
Gubernatorial Candidate	.006 (.011)	.006 (.011)	.006 (.011)
Vote Share	.487* (.222)	.470* (.219)	.448* (.218)
N	473	473	473

NOTES: Standard errors in parentheses. Models estimated using fixed-effects ordinary least squares (OLS) regression with robust standard errors clustered by state. $**p < .01$; $*p < .05$, two-tailed. Dependent variable is the deviation from proportionality. Unit of analysis is the state house delegation. At-large states excluded.

tical significance ($p = .085$), indicating that the Democrats actually benefited electorally from the 2000s round of redistricting, having suffered in the previous decade. This would seem to contrast with the popular narrative that declared the Republican Party the victors in the 2000s battle over district boundaries, and would seemingly indicate that whatever advantage the Republicans were able to secure in states where they controlled the process was more than offset by a pro-Democratic disproportionality in other states. Model 1, however, does not distinguish between different potential sources of these redistricting effects. For that, it is necessary to examine the effects of partisan gerrymandering compared to other forms of redistricting, which is the focus of models 2 and 3.

Perhaps the most surprising result in table 4.5 is that, controlling for other determinants of electoral disproportionality, the partisan redistricting variable in model 2 falls slightly short of statistical significance at the conventional .05 level, although it is significant at the .10 level. Taken as a whole, partisan control of the redistricting process does not appear to be associated with subsequent electoral disproportionality to the benefit of the gerrymandering party. What model 3 reveals however, is that this apparent lack of effect is an artifact of combining Democratic and Republican gerrymanders into a single category. When separate dummy variables are included, the effect of Democratic control of the redistricting process is negligible, while the coefficient for Republican gerrymandering is negative and statistically significant. This indicates that there was a greater level of pro-Republican electoral disproportionality in states where they controlled redistricting during the two most recent cycles.

Given that the Republican Party controlled redistricting in just two states during the 1990s, this effect would seem to almost exclusively result from the influence of the nine states in which they controlled the process in the subsequent decade. The effect size itself, however, is fairly modest: Republican control of redistricting was associated with a 10 percent change in the deviation from proportionality, meaning that the party would be expected to capture 10 percent more seats than their share of the popular vote would suggest. This is equivalent to a single extra seat won in a state with ten congressional districts, and two seats in a large state with twenty districts: not a negligible effect by any means, but much smaller than some of the more egregious examples of partisan gerrymandering would seem to suggest. When combining the effects of Republican gerrymandering and Democratic gerrymandering during this period, the overall impact declines to approximately 4 percent: enough to perhaps pick up an additional seat in a particularly large state, but not to produce large and enduring substantive effects on election outcomes across the board.

Of the other control variables, the only one that consistently reaches statistical significance is the measure of the aggregate Democratic vote share in the state. This indicates that there is indeed a "winner's bonus" present in the elections analyzed: the greater a party's vote share in the state, the more disproportional their seat percentage is expected to be. Contrary to expectations, neither the measure of apportionment or the small state dummy variable reach statistical significance in any of the models, indicating that these factors were not a significant source of disproportionality in House elections. Additionally, there is no evidence for the existence of coattail effects in the model, and the variable for the effects of uncontested districts is of only borderline statistical significance in one of the three models. Overall, the results from table 4.5 are largely in line with the theoretical expectation that the effects of partisan gerrymandering on subsequent election results would be less dramatic than the popular perception would indicate. Only Republican gerrymandering is statistically significant in any of the models, and while its substantive effect is not insubstantial, it is hardly dramatic.

Redistricting and Partisan Bias

Before proceeding to multivariate statistical analysis of the determinants of partisan bias, it seems prudent to first examine the underlying results from the JudgeIt simulations. The graphs in figures 4.3 and 4.4 illustrate the overall levels of partisan bias during the 1990s and 2000s redistricting cycles using the symmetry measure developed by Gelman and King (1994), disaggregated by the type of redistricting that occurred. This measure of partisan bias captures the degree of deviation from partisan symmetry when the average Democratic district vote is between 45 percent and 55 percent, a concept discussed earlier in this chapter. Positive values indicate a bias in favor of the Democratic Party—partisan bias of .05 on the scale corresponds to a situation when the Democrats win 5 percent more seats than they should under the symmetry standard—whereas negative values indicate similar bias in favor of the Republican Party. Figure 4.3 shows the level of partisan bias under different types of redistricting throughout the 1990s, whereas Figure 4.4 illustrates the same quantities of interest for the 2000s. For the 1990s redistricting cycle, there were too few states where redistricting was controlled by the Republican Party for the partisan bias statistic to be estimated, and so it is omitted from the figure.

The results in figure 3 indicate that control of redistricting had no significant effects on the overall level of partisan bias in subsequent elections during the 1990s. The lines representing Democratic gerrymandering, bipartisan redistricting, and redistricting by an independent commission are not meaningfully distinguishable from one another. Nevertheless, a small pro-Democratic bias is evident for the 1992 and 1994 elections in states where they controlled redistricting, and overall levels of partisan bias are very similar to the disproportionality results in the previous section. The Democrats received 12 percent more seats than the symmetry standard would predict in 1992, and 8 percent more in 1994. This is consistent with the story of Democratic legislatures in southern and border states that were desperately, but ultimately unsuccessfully, attempting to hold back the rising Republican electoral tide. The results also show that, not unexpectedly, neither bipartisan nor independent redistricting produced any significant bias in favor of either party.

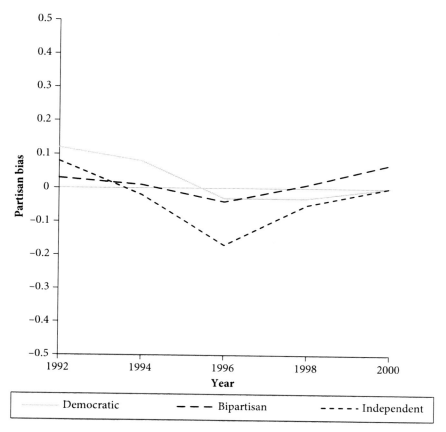

FIGURE 4.3. Control of Redistricting and Partisan Bias, 1992–2000

Note: Partisan bias calculated using Judgelt II, v.1.4.1 (Gelman, King, and Thomas 2012).

Figure 4.4, however, does indicate that the party in control of redistricting following the 2000 Census was able to gain a subsequent electoral advantage, and here that advantage in some instances is of greater substantive significance. Both Republicans and Democrats won approximately 12 percent more seats in congressional elections during the 2000s than the symmetry standard would have predicted, which is very similar to the aforementioned results for 1992 and 1994. The pro-Republican bias peaks at 22 percent in 2004 in states where they controlled redistricting, possibly because this is the election in which the effects of the mid-decade Texas redistricting are first felt, before declining to 17 percent in 2006 and approximately 10 percent in both 2008 and 2010. The pro-Democratic bias in states they controlled slowly increases from 2002 to 2006, before peaking at 23 percent in 2008, and then subsequently declining to

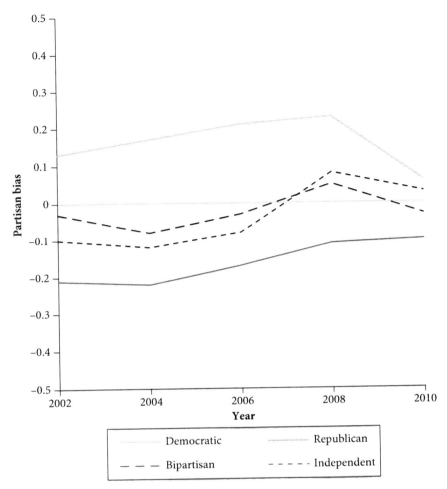

FIGURE 4.4.   Control of Redistricting and Partisan Bias, 2002–2010

Note: Partisan bias calculated using Judgelt II, v.1.4.1 (Gelman, King, and Thomas 2012).

6 percent in 2010, as the Republican landslide of that year saw them lose considerable strength at the ballot box.

These results provide mixed support for the theoretical expectations about the electoral effects of partisan gerrymandering. The effects were expected to be strongest in the initial elections after redistricting took place, and then to decline thereafter, which was true for the Democrats in the 1990s and the Republicans in the 2000s, but not for the Democrats in the 2000s. Overall, however, the figures seem to suggest that the degree of partisan bias in state delegations where partisan

gerrymandering has occurred is extremely similar to the electoral disproportionality estimates in the previous section. Nevertheless, they continue to support the conclusion that the effects of partisan gerrymandering, while real and in
some circumstances large enough to produce dramatic electoral effects, are
smaller overall than might be expected.

While the JudgeIt software was designed to analyze electoral systems at the
aggregate level, either an entire legislature or, as is the case here, a large group of
states within a legislature, it can also be used to calculate partisan bias within an
individual state house delegation. Since the JudgeIt estimation procedures necessarily limit this kind of analysis to only the largest states, this section serves as
more of a robustness check on the previous results than a separate and independent analysis. By developing such a measure, however, a multivariate model of
the determinants of partisan bias in these states can be estimated and its results
compared to the previously discussed effects of gerrymandering on electoral disproportionality. Using the same formula that was used to estimate partisan bias
in figures 4.3 and 4.4, a measure or partisan bias was estimated for the thirteen
states in which there were sufficient observations (California, Florida, Georgia,
Illinois, Indiana, Michigan, New Jersey, New York, North Carolina, Ohio, Pennsylvania, Texas, and Virginia). This yielded 143 total cases across the 1990s and 2000s
redistricting cycles, which is enough to conduct a similar statistical analysis as
was done with the disproportionality models in table 4.5. It also allows for
separate consideration of the question of whether the effects of redistricting
manifest themselves differently in the largest states with the most congressional
seats, compared to those that are much smaller. The results of this analysis are
presented in table 4.6.

The models in table 4.6 are a direct replication of those in table 4.5, replacing
the dependent variable of partisan electoral disproportionality with the JudgeIt
measure of partisan bias, and restricting the sample to only the aforementioned
thirteen large states. The results largely confirm the earlier findings in this chapter, albeit with a few interesting discrepancies and caveats. Once again, the overall vote share in a state was the largest single determinant of partisan bias in the
electoral system, and again the controls for coattail effects, uncontested districts,
and apportionment largely failed to reach statistical significance. Most notable,
however, is the fact that the effects of gerrymandering stand out much more
clearly in models 2 and 3 in table 4.6 than they did in the disproportionality
analyses in table 4.5. Not only does the variable for partisan gerrymandering
overall reach statistical significance at the .01 level (this variable was not
significant in the disproportionality models), but both the Democratic gerrymander and Republican gerrymander dummy variables are also highly significant ($p < .01$).

TABLE 4.6. Gerrymandering and Partisan Bias in U.S. House Elections, 1990–2010

	(1)	(2)	(3)
Time Trend	−.008**	−.004	−.004
	(.002)	(.003)	(.003)
1990s Redistricting	−.056	−.081	−.080
	(.051)	(.050)	(.050)
2000s Redistricting	.029	.046	.052
	(.046)	(.032)	(.031)
Partisan Gerrymander	—	.125**	—
		(.028)	
Democratic Gerrymander	—	—	.114**
			(.036)
Republican Gerrymander	—	—	−.135**
			(.035)
Apportionment	.111	.015	.018
	(.065)	(.055)	(.055)
Uncontested Districts	−.007	−.002	−.002
	(.005)	(.005)	(.005)
Senatorial Candidate	.004	.008	.008
	(.011)	(.012)	(.012)
Presidential Candidate	−.012	−.008	−.008
	(.012)	(.012)	(.011)
Gubernatorial Candidate	−.049**	−.047**	−.047**
	(.015)	(.013)	(.013)
Vote Share	1.125**	.676**	.667**
	(.256)	(.195)	(.194)
N	143	143	143

NOTES: Standard errors in parentheses. Models estimated using fixed-effects ordinary least squares (OLS) regression with robust standard errors clustered by state. $**p<.01$; $*p<.05$, two-tailed. Dependent variable is partisan bias, calculated using Judgelt II, v.1.4.1 (Gelman, King, and Thomas 2012). Unit of analysis is the state house delegation. At-large states excluded.

This would seem to indicate that partisan control of the redistricting process is of greater significance in large states than in smaller ones, and it would seem to be no coincidence that the cases that are usually cited as the most egregious examples of the gerrymandering of congressional districts, such as Florida, Pennsylvania, and Texas during the 2000s, are all large states with many districts, the boundaries of which line drawers can manipulate. Once again, however, as in figures 4.3 and 4.4, the substantive effects of gerrymandering on partisan bias appear to be relatively modest: Democrats won 11 percent more seats in states where they controlled redistricting than the symmetry standard would have predicted, whereas Republicans won 13.5 percent more seats than predicted in states where they were in control. Overall, partisan gerrymandering was associated with a 12.5 percent increase in the overall level of partisan bias in a state, which is somewhat higher than the 4 percent increase in disproportionality evidenced in table 4.5. This also supports the earlier contention that gerrymandering has somewhat larger effects in big states than it does in small ones, although more research is clearly needed to tease out the exact nature of these effects.

Redistricting and Probability of Democratic Party Victory

Table 4.7 presents the results of the district-level analysis of the effects of redistricting on subsequent election outcomes. The unit of analysis is the individual U.S House district, and the dependent variable is the probability of the Democratic Party candidate winning the election in that district in a given year. The results for all House elections from 1990 to 2010 were pooled together, yielding 4,709 cases for analysis after at-large districts were excluded. As with tables 4.5 and 4.6, model 1 represents the baseline model before the effects of control of redistricting are introduced. Here, the probability of Democratic victory in a given district was modeled as a function of campaign expenditures, using the spending ratio variable described earlier, the normalized presidential vote in the district, the lagged Democratic vote share from the previous election, and the incumbency status of the candidates. Though the dependent variable is dichotomous, for simplicity and to ease interpretation, a linear probability model was estimated with standard errors clustered by state, although the results are substantially unchanged when replicated using logit or probit models. This is similar to the estimation approach used by Friedman and Holden (2009), who also adopt a linear probability model to analyze the determinants of the probability of incumbent reelection. Each of the models also includes state fixed effects, a linear time trend, and a step function for each individual redistricting cycle. The models overall perform extremely well, predicting the outcomes of elections in individual districts with a high degree of accuracy, and achieving a significant proportional reduction in error over the modal outcome. Model 2 also includes the measure of partisan gerrymandering overall, while model 3 introduces separate dummy variables for Democratic and Republican gerrymandering.

The results are remarkably similar to those in the earlier aggregate-level analysis that examined the effects of redistricting on electoral disproportionality and partisan bias in state house delegations. Each of the control variables works as expected, with the probability of a Democratic victory in a particular district being significantly greater when the Democratic candidate outspends his or her Republican opponent, when the district itself votes Democratic in presidential

TABLE 4.7. Gerrymandering and Probability of Democratic Victory in U.S. House Elections, 1990–2010

	(1)	(2)	(3)
Time Trend	−.002**	−.002*	−.002
	(.000)	(.001)	(.002)
1990s Redistricting	−.020	−.024	−.021
	(.013)	(.014)	(.013)
2000s Redistricting	.018	.018	.019
	(.013)	(.013)	(.013)
Partisan Gerrymander	—	.011	—
		(.008)	
Democratic Gerrymander	—	—	−.012
			(.011)
Republican Gerrymander	—	—	−.040**
			(.014)
Spending Ratio	.254**	.253**	.253**
	(.014)	(.014)	(.014)
Presidential Vote	.003**	.003**	.003**
	(.001)	(.001)	(.001)
Lagged Vote Share	.002**	.002**	.002**
	(.000)	(.00)	(.000)
Incumbency	.202**	.202**	.201**
	(.013)	(.013)	(.013)
N	4,709	4,709	4,709

NOTES: Standard errors in parentheses. Models estimated using fixed-effects ordinary least squares (OLS) regression with robust standard errors clustered by state. **$p < .01$; *$p < .05$, two-tailed. Dependent variable is the probability that the Democratic candidate wins the election. Unit of analysis is the House district. At-large states excluded.

elections, when the Democratic candidate was successful in the previous election in that district, and when a Democratic incumbent was running in the election. The effect of the overall measure incorporating both Democratic and Republican gerrymandering, while in the expected direction, again fails to achieve statistical significance.

Again, however, this is revealed in model 3 to be a function of the fact that Democratic gerrymandering is not associated with any greater likelihood of Democratic victory in subsequent elections. The coefficient itself is actually negative, indicating that Democratic candidates were in fact harmed in states where their party had controlled the redistricting process, although the effect is not statistically significant. Republican gerrymandering, however, is associated with a statistically significant decrease in the probability that Democratic candidates will win seats in subsequent elections. This would indicate that those Republicans in the state legislature responsible for line drawing in these states were able to successfully use that control to benefit their fellow partisans at the congressional level. As with the electoral disproportionality results discussed earlier, control of redistricting overall seems to have significantly benefited the Republican Party in the 2000s, but not the Democrats in that decade or either party in the 1990s.

Because the dependent variable is binary, the gerrymandering coefficients can be interpreted as the percentage increase in the probability of Democratic victory, in a way similar to the previous analyses of the effects of redistricting on the Democratic percentage of seats won in the state delegation. The coefficient of −.04 on the Republican gerrymandering variable therefore indicates that, holding all else equal, Democratic candidates were 4 percent less likely to win elections in states where the Republican Party controlled redistricting than in states where they did not, enough to make a significant difference in a particularly close race. Though it does not reach statistical significance, the effect of a Democratic gerrymandering in the model is to increase Democratic candidates' likelihood of victory by 1.2 percent, meaning that the overall difference between a Democratic gerrymander and a Republican gerrymander is a change of slightly greater than 5 percent in the likelihood of Democratic candidates emerging victorious at the district level. Across a reasonably large state, this would seem to be sufficient to flip one or two districts from the party targeted by the gerrymander to the party implementing it, an effect size that is consistent with the earlier analyses of the effects of redistricting at the state delegation level.

Conclusions

The theory of constrained redistricting predicted that partisan gerrymandering would indeed produce significant electoral advantages for the gerrymandering party, but that these effects would be smaller than would be necessary to shut the other party out of the political process entirely under the Supreme Court's *Bandemer* standard. Indeed, it was also expected that the effects of partisan gerrymandering, while significant, would be smaller than popular perception of gerrymandering enabling parties to effectively rig the results of future elections would suggest. These expectations appear to be largely borne out in the data. Overall, across multiple operationalizations of the dependent variable and two different levels of analysis, the results presented in this chapter have been remarkably consistent. Though partisan gerrymandering can be an effective tool for improving a party's subsequent electoral fortunes in certain contexts, as evidenced by the consistently statistically significant effects of Republican gerrymandering in each of the models, its impact does not seem to be felt across the board. The effects of Democratic gerrymandering were not statistically significant in any of the models, with the exception of the restricted sample analysis focusing only on large states. This was the case despite the fact that the Democratic Party was in control of the redistricting process in fourteen states during the 1990s cycle and nine during the 2000s cycle. There is also some evidence in the partisan bias analysis and raw seat-change numbers that the effects of gerrymandering are felt most strongly in the first few elections after redistricting occurs, and less so later in the ten-year cycle. However, the evidence for this is less than fully conclusive, and further research is clearly needed to more fully differentiate between those circumstances in which gerrymandering is likely to be more effective and those in which it is not.

Based on the evidence, partisan gerrymandering appears to be most effective in larger states where there is greater opportunity to manipulate district boundaries; in situations where a state has gained congressional seats as a result of reapportionment; where there is not an electoral climate of existing bias toward the gerrymandering party; and where there is a history of partisan gerrymandering in the state by the opposing party. This combination of circumstances may produce a perfect storm, as occurred in Texas in 2003, when the Republicans were finally able to gain unified control of state government after decades in the wilderness. The six seats the Republican Party gained in Texas in 2004 were only one less than they were able to gain in total in 2002 in all of the remaining states where they controlled redistricting. In such circumstances, partisan gerrymandering may allow for a much quicker and more effective "correction" of existing partisan bias than redistricting by supposedly neutral groups such as independent commissions or the courts, which tend to be more resistant to making dramatic changes to existing boundaries.

The "neutral" redistricting plan drawn up by the panel of federal judges for the 2002 election in Texas is a good example of this, while the 2003 Republican gerrymander actually served to decrease overall partisan bias in Texas's congressional delegation. The situation we saw in Texas in 2003, however, and in several other large states where the Republicans were in control of redistricting following the 2000 Census, represents the exception rather than the norm. The alternate side of the coin is the predicament in which the Democratic Party found itself in the South during the 1990s, where controlling the redistricting process and attempting to use it to insulate its existing electoral strength actually produced worse outcomes for the party in subsequent elections than if it had been forced to compromise on line drawing.

The results also show that parties would do best to avoid overreaching when attempting to implement a partisan gerrymander. Producing an efficient gerrymander requires capturing as many seats as possible with small majorities, and these manufactured majorities are very unstable. They are likely to erode over time as populations shift and the underlying distribution of voters moves away from that which formed the basis of the original boundaries. Artificial majorities created by gerrymandering also appear to be very susceptible to national electoral shocks. For instance, the partisan gerrymander implemented by the Republican Party in Pennsylvania allowed the party to increase its seat total from a roughly even split to a 12–7 majority in 2002 and 2004. But Pennsylvania is a state split relatively evenly between Democrats and Republicans, and so carving up the electoral map to manufacture a majority necessarily made that majority unstable. As a result, the Democrats were able to capture four marginal seats from the Republicans in 2006, followed by another in 2008, and this allegedly pervasive and undemocratic subversion of the will of the voters had disappeared within four years of its first electoral effects, although the Republicans were able to win back these seats and more in their 2010 midterm landslide.

Of the thirty seats the Democrats were able to win from the Republicans to take control of the House of Representatives in 2006, eleven came from the seven states in which Republicans had controlled redistricting after the 2000 Census, followed by another eight in 2008. Similarly, in the Republican victory in 2010, thirty-four of the sixty-three seats they captured came from partisan gerrymandering states, although a greater share of these, twenty-three, came from states where the Republicans had controlled redistricting, whereas eleven came from states where the Democrats had been in control. The theory that the utility of partisan redistricting is constrained by a combination of the nature of gerrymandering itself, the electoral climate in which partisan redistricting is most likely to take place, and demographic factors that dilute its effects appears to be generally supported by the evidence from the two most recent redistricting cycles.

REDISTRICTING, ELECTORAL RESPONSIVENESS, AND DEMOCRACY

American politics has long been characterized by an inherent hostility to organized political interests. More than a century after the Founding Fathers demonstrated a deep general distrust of interest groups and party government and aimed at "curing the mischiefs of faction" (Madison 1787), the Progressive Era reformers mounted a concerted campaign to take politics out of the hands of politicians. By promoting direct democracy in the form of the citizen ballot initiative, they created a mechanism for lawmaking that bypasses the people's elected representatives in government entirely. Even today, studies continue to demonstrate that Americans find political conflict distasteful; view politicians as selfish and divisive; and see disagreement, deliberation, and compromise as symptoms of something terribly wrong with democracy (Hibbing and Theiss-Morse 2002). Opinion polls consistently find support for proposals that weaken parties, limit the power of government, and take decision making out of the arena of partisan politics (Hibbing and Theiss-Morse 1995), while popular accounts often lament the influence that nonspecific "special interests" have on elected officials. This hostility toward all forms of party conflict is no more evident than in the redistricting process, which exhibits many if not all of the characteristics that Americans find so distasteful about politics.

And yet for decades, many political scientists have put forward both empirical and normative arguments in favor of the two-party system, emphasizing in particular the virtues of accountability, responsiveness, and representation that are a by-product of robust party competition. As E. E. Schattschneider (1942, 1) succinctly stated: "political parties created democracy and . . . modern democracy is unthinkable save in terms of the parties." The emphasis here is often on the benefits of competitive elections for a democratic system, from V. O. Key's analysis in *Southern Politics* (1955) and *American State Politics* (1956), which identified two-party competition as a necessary condition for the proper functioning of democracy, to more recent studies that have demonstrated a link between competitive elections and positive democratic externalities such as turnout, citizen interest, and involvement in politics (Blais and Dobrzynska 1998; Franklin 2004). Indeed, an entire American Political Science Association (APSA) committee report was dedicated to moving the United States "toward a more responsible two-party system" (1950), something that has been reiterated in numerous subsequent studies as part of the APSA Responsible Parties Project, which ran from 1950 to 2000.

It must be noted, however, that the normative view that competitive elections serve to enhance democracy and improve representation is not without its detractors. Some studies have made the counterintuitive argument that uncompetitive legislative elections are actually a good thing for democracy because they maximize the share of voters in a district whose political preferences match those of their representative. At the same time, lopsided electoral margins serve to minimize the proportion of the electorate who are disappointed on election day because their preferred candidate lost. And, as critics of competitive elections such as Brunell (2008) have noted, voters who support a losing candidate exhibit lower levels of satisfaction not only with their own representative, but with Congress as a whole, and a greater propensity to express dissatisfaction with government in general. Though Brunell's argument is a refreshing and provocative challenge to the conventional wisdom, it is, however, by no means the consensus viewpoint among political scientists, for whom political competition has always had and continues to occupy a privileged position in the canons of American democracy. This attitude is not simply based on normative considerations: many empirical studies have uncovered links between competitive elections and a number of positive democratic attributes (Lipsitz 2011).

More recent research published since Brunell's 2008 book has also to some extent undermined the conclusions he reached. Canon (2009) points out that many of the negative effects on voter satisfaction uncovered by Brunell are substantively extremely small, while others have demonstrated that they do not tend to endure much beyond the election itself (Evans 2013). Another study found that voters in competitive states not only have higher levels of interest in politics and knowledge about the policy positions of their elected representatives, but they were also more likely to hold them accountable for those positions come election time (Jones 2013). Other research has shown that district-level competitiveness, measured using campaign spending data, is associated with greater attention to news coverage about the election (Bowler and Donovan 2011). Finally, it has also been demonstrated that these positive effects of electoral competition endure beyond the duration of the campaign itself (Evans, Ensley, and Carmines 2014), and that this link between competition and citizen engagement and participation is strongest among those who serve to benefit from it most: those with lower levels of education and income (Flavin and Shufeldt 2015). Despite Brunell's findings, the consensus in the political science literature remains that the positive effects of a competitive electoral landscape outweigh the negative.

To be sure, competitiveness for the sake of competitiveness is not something that should be a major driving force behind any call for specific electoral or institutional reforms. When taken to extremes, ultracompetitive electoral districts are likely to foster instability in a political system, where control of the levers of power hinges on idiosyncratic factors specific to individual campaigns and other largely random effects. Nevertheless, a certain critical mass of competitive districts in a legislature or state is important for other reasons, most notably because it serves as a prerequisite for a quality that arguably is essential for the proper functioning of a democratic system: electoral responsiveness. Responsiveness refers to the extent to which the electoral system responds to shifts in voter preferences, by translating those preferences into changes in the composition of the legislature. A highly unresponsive system will serve to insulate incumbent politicians against changes in voter sentiment, while a highly responsive system will see even small shifts in the popular vote produce a significant reallocation of legislative seats. And, while too much responsiveness in an electoral system can certainly be a bad thing, its virtue as a mechanism for democratic accountability is abundantly clear. Citing the research of Ferejohn (1977) and others, Gelman and King (1994, 544) conclude that "scholars of American politics almost uniformly take the normative position that higher values of responsiveness indicate a healthier democracy," contrasting this with the preference for proportional representation among scholars from other countries.

Researchers have long been observing a steady decline in the competitiveness of House elections and an increase in polarization at both the elite and mass level, with the number of seats in play seemingly shrinking with each electoral cycle (Abramowitz, Alexander, and Gunning 2006). While the ideal level of responsiveness for effective democratic self-governance is an empirical question that remains to be definitively answered, the recent experience of the 2012 election, where the Republican Party was able to hold on to a thirty-three-seat majority in the House despite losing the popular vote to the Democrats by 1.2 percent, a margin of almost 1.5 million votes, suggests that concerns over the level of responsiveness in the U.S. electoral system are not unfounded. This very case is made by Lipsitz (2011), who argues that U.S. elections could benefit from being more competitive, although crucially, not too much more so. Closely contested elections, she argues, while in many ways stressful for both the candidates and voters who participate in them, are actually a healthy thing for democracy because they foster an environment that allows citizens to make more informed decisions when choosing their elected representatives. She concludes with a call for reforms to enhance competition in U.S. elections, providing an important counterpoint to Brunell's thesis regarding the deleterious consequences of competitive elections.

While the ongoing normative and empirical debate among political scientists about the virtues of electoral competition obviously will not be resolved here, it is clear that any analysis of the effects of redistricting generally, and partisan gerrymandering specifically, must take into account the implications that control of redistricting has for electoral competitiveness and responsiveness. To demonstrate, as chapter 4 does, that partisan gerrymandering has significant but relatively minor effects on partisan bias is not sufficient to defend it against charges that it undermines democracy if, as many critics allege, it still has a deleterious effect on electoral competition. The approach taken in this chapter, therefore, is to investigate, through systematic empirical analysis, the effect that control of the redistricting process has on the competitiveness of U.S. House districts, seat change in Congress, and the overall responsiveness of the system to changes in voter preferences.

Theoretical Perspectives

The mechanism by which an electoral system is responsive to changes in voter preferences, by allocating seats in the legislature in a way that is consistent with the overall partisan swing, is dependent on the competitiveness of the individual districts within that jurisdiction. This can be illustrated by a simple hypothetical example. In any given U.S. House election where there is a partisan swing in the popular vote, for example a 5 percent swing from the Republican Party to the Democratic Party, the number of seats the party gains from that swing will depend a great deal on district-level competitiveness. Seats that are more competitive are much more likely to yield enough of a shift in the district-level vote from one party to the other for the seat to change hands than seats that were previously uncompetitive or uncontested. Although a party may capture a number of open seats, its ability to pick up seats from its opponents in response to a popular vote increase is also dependent on a number of incumbents losing their reelection bids. If none of the seats in a jurisdiction are competitive, even large swings in the popular vote may be insufficient to produce a significant degree of seat change, indicating a system that is not responsive to the will of the electorate. How, then, might we expect redistricting to affect the levels of competitiveness and responsiveness in subsequent elections?

The redistricting process in the United States can be characterized as a tension between two competing priorities: partisan advantage and incumbent protection (Campbell 1996; King and Gelman 1991). These, in turn, must also operate within constraints such as the protection of minority groups and other legal requirements. Partisan advantage refers to the desire of the political parties to use the redistricting process to maximize their share of legislative seats. Incumbent protection refers to the desire of incumbent candidates and their parties to use the redistricting process to protect the seats that they already hold, and to make the future reelection bids by current members of the legislature easier. Whenever congressional district boundaries are redrawn in response to a decennial census, the result necessarily represents a compromise between partisan advantage and incumbent protection. Exactly where the balance is struck between the two and how much emphasis is placed either on gaining partisan advantage in Congress or protecting the seats of existing incumbents can have significant consequences for electoral competition. While redistricting as a whole has been shown to have little or no effect on the overall level of competition in U.S. House elections (Abramowitz, Alexander, and Gunning 2006), it is possible that this general finding obscures important differences between partisan and bipartisan gerrymandering in terms of their consequences for competitiveness and electoral responsiveness.

Theory predicts that implementing a gerrymander that systematically benefits one party at the expense of the other may lead to greater responsiveness than in situations where divided state government necessitates partisan compromise on the redrawing of district boundaries. In the absence of unified partisan control of both the legislative and executive branches of state government, it is extremely difficult for a redistricting plan to be passed that has any significant overall partisan advantage. Any attempt by one party to implement a partisan gerrymander will likely be met with resistance from the other party, which, as a veto player, has the ability to block any redistricting plan it finds objectionable. In cases of divided state government, the parties generally must agree on neutral and nonpartisan criteria for redrawing district boundaries, and in the absence of significant prospects for gaining additional seats through gerrymandering, parties generally approach redistricting with the goal of protecting what they already hold. Incumbent protection therefore becomes the usual method by which parties compromise on redistricting in order to produce a mutually beneficial plan. States with bipartisan redistricting generally tend to redistrict in a way that entrenches incumbents from both parties, thus leading to lower levels of electoral competition and responsiveness.

This type of redistricting not only tends to increase the odds of electoral defeat for incumbents of the party not in control of the process but also often hurts some incumbents of the party that is in control. Partisan redistricting seeks to create an electoral advantage by targeting incumbents of the opposing party. This can be done in several ways. The most controversial method is known as pairing, whereby boundaries are redrawn in such a way that two incumbents of the same party are paired together in a single district. The intention of the party implementing the gerrymander is not only to force two opposing incumbents to run against each other by drawing the residence of one into the other's district, but also to create an open seat elsewhere that can be captured by the party implementing the gerrymander. This has the simultaneous advantage of both unseating an opposing partisan and also allowing the party to pick up an additional seat without having to defeat an incumbent in the process, thus negating the significant electoral advantages of incumbency. Though extremely effective, this type of gerrymandering generally happens most frequently when a state has lost congressional seats as a result of reapportionment, thus making some degree of pairing inevitable. In general, the federal courts have frowned on the use of pairing that is obviously intended to discriminate against one party, and the practice is more widespread when parties are redrawing the boundaries for state legislative districts. Extensive pairing is generally not practical in congressional redistricting due to the smaller number of districts and their increased geographical size.

The second method makes use of cracking and packing to target opposing partisans. A party implementing a gerrymander will pack its opponent's supporters into the districts of a few incumbents, while cracking the supporters of other incumbents whom it wants to target. These targeted incumbents are drawn into districts where they will face competitive elections against strong challengers from the party implementing the gerrymander, which hopes to unseat as many opposing incumbents as possible with the maximum possible vote efficiency. This tactic is evident in the 2003 Texas redistricting, where white Democratic incumbents were targeted by the Republican plan, which cracked their districts and forced them into competitive races, whereas minority Democratic incumbents were packed into safe districts in order to avoid allegations of racial gerrymandering, which might have made the plan unconstitutional under the Voting Rights Act. Despite this, parts of the Texas plan were struck down by the U.S. Supreme Court for Voting Rights Act violations in *League of United Latin American Citizens v. Perry* (2006).

However, the use of cracking and packing to target opposing partisans also has the added effect of making some incumbents of the party that controls redistricting increasingly vulnerable. The reason for this is that when the opposing party's districts are cracked, those blocs of support must be drawn into other districts. If the redistricting party is prevented by geographical constraints from packing these blocs into supermajority districts where the opposing party will waste large numbers of surplus votes, then incumbents of the controlling party must have their district boundaries modified to incorporate these opposing partisans. This makes these districts more competitive and increases the chances that the controlling party may lose these seats in future elections. Attempts to gain a partisan advantage through maximizing vote efficiency will therefore necessarily hurt incumbents of the party that controls redistricting by making their districts less safe, while at the same time increasing the overall level of electoral competition and, by implication, the responsiveness of the electoral system.

The third and most subtle method by which partisan gerrymandering makes incumbents more electorally vulnerable is known as dislocation. This method attempts to weaken opposing party incumbents without necessarily attempting to unseat them through targeted cracking or pairing. Dislocation involves shifting the core of the incumbent's district from one area to another without significantly diluting the electoral strength of the opposing party. The intention is to force the incumbent to run for reelection in a district with a significantly different geographical basis, thus weakening the traditional incumbency advantages of name recognition and constituency service. The incumbent is therefore either redrawn into an entirely new district, or has significant areas carved from his or her existing district and replaced with other geographical localities.

The end result is that the incumbent is forced to run in a dramatically different geographical area. This robs the opposing party of the positive effects of incumbency and the personal vote, since voters in these new areas are less familiar with the incumbent, and they are unable to rely as much on the traditional electoral advantages of "bringing home the bacon." Indeed, any significant shift in electoral boundaries, as would likely happen under a partisan gerrymander, will be an impediment to incumbent candidates, while incumbents tend to benefit significantly from the status quo due to their ability to maintain name recognition, a process known as "securing the district" (Zaller 1994). The extent to which a redistricting plan emphasizes incumbent protection and partisan advantage therefore has significant implications for the competitiveness of House elections in that state.

To summarize, there are several reasons why we might expect redistricting that places a greater emphasis on partisan advantage than on incumbent protection to produce more competitive seats. Partisan gerrymandering is generally accomplished by two principal strategies that act in tandem with one other to maximize the effective votes of one party while minimizing those of another. Redistricters may break up the targeted party's geographical bases of support into several different districts, thus diluting its votes and reducing its efficiency. These supporters are thereby unable to vote in sufficient concentrations to win the individual seats into which they are divided, even though overall they may represent a significant enough voting bloc to warrant representation. They may also combine the targeted party's geographical bases of support into a few supermajority districts, thus wasting significant numbers of its votes in a few overwhelming victories and allowing the other party to capture neighboring seats. Partisan gerrymandering is generally accomplished using a combination of these tactics to pack some of the targeted party's voters into districts where they constitute a large majority, while cracking the rest of its voters into districts where they are only slightly in the minority. The intended effect is for the targeted party to win a few districts by large majorities with many wasted votes, whereas the gerrymandering party wins a large number of districts by small majorities with a highly efficient vote distribution.

The inherent dangers in this practice are immediately evident: the greater the reward a party seeks to gain from partisan gerrymandering the greater the risk it must take in implementing it. The capacity for a gerrymander to distort election results depends on the ability of the party controlling redistricting to capture seats by marginal majorities and hold on to them in subsequent elections. The more effective a partisan gerrymander seeks to be, therefore, and the more it focuses on redrawing district boundaries to maximize partisan advantage rather than incumbent protection, the more competitive districts should be created. However, the greater focus on incumbent protection under bipartisan redistricting, whereby the parties compromise by agreeing to protect incumbents on both sides, should lead to fewer competitive districts since incumbents are drawn safe districts that assure them a large enough margin of victory to be insulated from external electoral shocks. The increased number of competitive districts in states with partisan gerrymandering should increase responsiveness by making it more likely that districts a party is able to capture by small electoral margins through redistricting will change hands in response to a national swing away from that party in subsequent elections.

In their comprehensive study of the effects of redistricting on state legislative elections between 1968 and 1988, Gelman and King (1994, 548) found that redistricting, whether partisan or bipartisan, serves to increase responsiveness compared to an electoral system without redistricting because it "creates uncertainty by shaking up the political system." The implication of the theory of constrained redistricting is that partisan redistricting should provide a greater "shock" to the system than bipartisan redistricting, thus translating into a larger increase in electoral competition and responsiveness. The next section seeks to test this hypothesis empirically.

Data and Methods

The analysis of the effects of partisan redistricting on electoral competition in this chapter follows a similar blueprint to the previous analysis of partisan bias, focusing on the two most recent fully completed ten-year redistricting cycles. The effects of redistricting on the results of U.S. House elections from 1990 to 2010 were assessed at both the aggregate state delegation level and the individual district level, and multiple operationalizations of the dependent variable were considered in order to bolster the robustness of the results. States with only a single at-large congressional district were again excluded from the analysis, since redistricting only has the potential to influence responsiveness when congressional boundaries are redrawn, and the modeling approach was based on that used by Friedman and Holden (2009) in their study of redistricting and incumbency. If bias and responsiveness are simply two sides of the same coin when it comes to the electoral effects of redistricting, we should expect the results of this analysis to be highly consistent with those in chapter 4. Wherever we find evidence of partisan gerrymandering creating significant partisan bias and electoral disproportionality, we should also see it leading to greater competitiveness and electoral responsiveness.

Dependent Variables

The first dependent variables used in the empirical analysis were district-level measures of the competitiveness of U.S House elections. As discussed in the previous section, a certain critical mass of competitive seats in an electoral system is necessary for that system to respond effectively to changes in voter sentiment. There are two basic approaches to measuring the competitiveness of legislative districts, and both are utilized here. The first, and more intuitive, is electoral competitiveness, which measures the competitiveness of a district based on the actual results of elections that have taken place there. The second, more difficult approach is latent competitiveness, which attempts to capture the underlying competitiveness of a district absent the confounding effects of factors like incumbency and campaign spending that also affect election outcomes. Abramowitz, Alexander, and Gunning (2006) measure the latent competitiveness of U.S.

House districts based on the district presidential vote. The district presidential vote captures how Democratic or Republican an individual district is in a way that is exogenous to the results of actual House elections. However, simply using the raw district presidential vote percentage as a measure of district competition is problematic since it varies significantly from election to election depending on the relative fortunes of the parties' presidential candidates. So a perfectly competitive district may appear to be more Democratic in a year such as 2008, where a Democrat is victorious in the presidential election, while appearing more Republican in a year like 2004, where a Republican wins the White House. Because of this, the measure must be purged of its interelection variation in order to be a reliable estimate of district partisanship.

The approach taken by Abramowitz, Alexander, and Gunning to measure district competitiveness in a way that is comparable across elections is to use the normalized two-party district presidential vote. This is calculated by subtracting the Democratic presidential candidate's percentage of the national two-party vote from their two-party vote percentage in each individual House district. Districts that are more Democratic than the nation as a whole thus take on positive values of the normalized vote, whereas districts that are more Republican take on negative values. Using the normalized vote approach, they conclude that redistricting has had little or no effect on the decline of competition in U.S. House elections.

While the district presidential vote is a good indicator of how Democratic or Republican a district is when compared to the nation as a whole, it is less useful as a proxy for district competitiveness. Campbell (1996) argues that this approach makes an assumption of universal electoral swing across all districts that cannot be justified based on observed electoral behavior. The reason for this is that there is no intuitive neutral point for calculating the deviation of a district's normalized presidential vote from parity. The 50 percent mark of the two-party vote provides an ideal neutral point for calculating electoral competitiveness: the more the result deviates from a fifty-fifty split, the less competitive the election is. However, there is no corresponding point of comparison for the normalized presidential vote since the neutral point of the normalized district presidential vote is dependent on the national presidential vote. Districts are compared based on the extent to which they deviate from the national vote, but the zero point, where the district vote is exactly equal to the national vote, does not necessarily imply a competitive district.

To use such a measure would be to assume that if the Democratic presidential candidate receives 53 percent of the national two-party vote and 53 percent of the two-party vote in district X, then district X is perfectly competitive. Yet this is predicated on the relationship between the composition of the electorate and the presidential candidate's vote share being the same in district X as it is in the nation as a whole, something that is extremely unlikely to hold true across the board. Despite its problems, considering the effects of redistricting on latent competitiveness provides a useful starting point for assessing the overall relationship between partisan redistricting and electoral responsiveness, and so it is used as the dependent variable in the first set of empirical analyses. Of greater interest, however, is whether the effects of gerrymandering translate into more electoral competitiveness and seat change, the prerequisites for a responsive electoral system, once actual elections are held in these districts.

The second set of empirical analyses therefore examine the effects of redistricting on the actual observed competitiveness of House elections that take place following redistricting, while controlling for other factors that are expected to affect electoral competitiveness. In this way, the effects of redistricting on actual election outcomes can be isolated from these potentially confounding factors, providing a better understanding of the implications of control of redistricting for the competitiveness of subsequent elections. Electoral competitiveness was measured as the extent to which the two-party vote in each House district deviated from parity in a particular election, reflected in the 50 percent threshold that a candidate would need to exceed in order to win the seat. So districts in which the outcome of a congressional election was close to a 50–50 tie between the Democratic and Republican candidates are considered the most competitive, while competitiveness decreases as the two-party vote percentage deviates from this neutral point. The least competitive district is one where either the Democratic or Republican party candidate wins 100 percent of the two-party vote. Following the literature, uncontested districts were dealt with by imputing a value of 75 percent of the vote for the winning party and 25 percent for the losing party, rather than excluding them from the analysis altogether (Kastellec, Gelman, and Chandler 2008). To obtain an intuitive measure of the electoral competitiveness (EC) of a district (i), whereby higher values indicate greater levels of electoral competition whereas lower values indicate less-competitive districts, the following formula was used. All calculations were based on the Democratic share of the two-party vote in the district ($V\%_i$):

$$EC_i = 100 - |50 - V\%_i|$$

This measure ranges from a score of 50 for the least competitive district to a score of 100 for the most competitive district, and with a 1 percent increase in competitiveness indicative of a 1 percent movement in the two-party vote percentage in the direction of parity. A district where the Democratic candidate won 55 percent of the two-party vote would be coded as a 95 on this competitiveness scale, indicating that a 5 percent change in the popular vote would be necessary to move that district to the 50 percent threshold. Similarly, a district where the Democratic candidate won 60 percent of the popular vote percentage would correspond to a score of 90 in competitiveness, indicating a 5 percent reduction in competitiveness compared to the first hypothetical district, or a 5 percent movement in the two-party popular vote away from parity. However, the competitiveness of districts and the responsiveness of an electoral system are not synonymous with one another: a competitive district may nevertheless produce uncompetitive elections due to the influence of incumbency, campaign spending, or other factors idiosyncratic to a particular election campaign. Similarly, a district that is not really competitive may appear so for one or more electoral cycles due some of these same factors, such as the influence of presidential coattails or turnout variation between midterm and presidential elections. It is important, therefore, to consider whether the effects of partisan gerrymandering on district-level competitiveness translate into an influence on overall electoral responsiveness.

Another key prerequisite for a responsive electoral system is the ability for seats in the legislature to change hands between the two major parties from election to election. It would matter little if partisan gerrymandering were found to increase the overall competitiveness of House districts if, despite these effects, the vast majority of seats were still too safe to switch control in response to a shift in the popular vote. For this reason, the third operationalization of the dependent variable at the district level is the probability of legislative seats changing hands during an election, either from the Democrats to the Republicans or the Republicans to the Democrats. This variable was coded as 1 if a given seat was won by a different party than controlled it following the results of the previous election, and 0 otherwise. Taken together, electoral competition and seat change provide the key district-level ingredients for greater electoral responsiveness at the aggregate level. If partisan gerrymandering is found to have a positive effect on each of these indicators, we would expect to see those effects translating into an increase of the responsiveness of the electoral system overall.

This final step in the causal chain between redistricting and responsiveness is the focus of the fourth operationalization of the dependent variable. This utilizes the partisan symmetry standard described previously, from which an overall measure of electoral responsiveness can also be derived. Unlike the previous measures of latent competitiveness, electoral competitiveness, and seat change, electoral responsiveness was measured at the aggregate state delegation level rather than at the level of the individual House district. It can then be used to compare the level of responsiveness in states where different types of redistricting has taken place. The measure of electoral responsiveness used in this part of the analysis was developed by Gelman and King (1994, 544), and captures the degree to which the partisan composition of the legislature as a whole changes in response to shifts in voter preferences. It is defined as "the change in the expected seat proportion given a small change in the vote proportion, from slightly more Democratic than the average district vote to slightly more Republican."

In a highly responsive legislature, wherein many districts are competitive, a small swing in the popular vote from one party to the other will translate into a large number of seats changing hands, whereas in a legislature with a much lower level of electoral responsiveness and containing many fewer competitive districts, a small swing in the popular vote from one party to the other will lead to many fewer seats switching control. Following Gelman and King, JudgeIt was used to measure electoral responsiveness, which was calculated separately for states with partisan redistricting, states with bipartisan redistricting, and states with redistricting conducted by an independent commission. As a further robustness check, this measure of responsiveness was also calculated at the individual state-delegation level for the same subset of large states as in chapter 4, for use in a multivariate regression model of the determinants of electoral responsiveness in state house delegations.

Independent Variables

The main independent variables of interest are the measures of control of redistricting. These variables were operationalized based on the classification of each state redistricting as partisan, bipartisan, independent, or judicial. Dummy variables were included for states in which one political party was in unilateral control of the redistricting process, states in which redistricting was conducted by the courts, and states where redistricting was undertaken by an independent or nonpartisan commission. Therefore, the omitted category in the analysis was states in which redistricting was bipartisan, and the models allow for estimation of the effect of partisan redistricting, redistricting by commission, and redistricting by the courts, on the four different operationalizations of the dependent variable in comparison to this baseline category. In addition to the combined measure of partisan gerrymandering, separate dummy variables were also created for Democratic gerrymandering and Republican gerrymandering, which were also compared to the baseline category of bipartisan redistricting.

There is significant reason to expect that electoral competitiveness and seat change will be affected by other factors besides redistricting (Abramowitz, Alexander, and Gunning 2006). It has been well established in the literature on congressional elections that campaign expenditures are a major determinant of the outcomes of House races (Ansolabehere and Gerber 1994; Erikson and Palfrey

1998; Kenny and McBurnett 1994). For this reason, the models also control for campaign spending by the major party candidates. It is expected that districts are more likely to be marginal when both the Democratic and Republican candidates spend approximately equal amounts on their campaigns than when one candidate significantly outspends his or her opponent. The models include a measure of the absolute value of the spending ratio, or the extent to which one candidate in the district was outspending his or her opponent, and by how much. This was calculated using the approach outlined by Gierzynski and Breaux (1993) and Seabrook (2010). Utilizing the spending ratio rather than candidates' expenditure totals helps account for potential endogeneity between spending and competitiveness. While both candidates are expected to increase their spending in anticipation of a competitive election, the ratio between the Democratic and Republican candidates' expenditures is not expected to be significantly altered. This variable is expected to have a negative effect on electoral competitiveness and seat change. Finally, a control variable was included to capture the effects of incumbency, coded as 1 if an incumbent representative was running in the general election in a district, and 0 otherwise. Given the extremely high incumbent reelection rate in House elections, this variable is also expected to have a negative effect on electoral competitiveness and seat change. All of the models include a time trend, step functions for each redistricting cycle, and state fixed effects, and are estimated with robust standard errors clustered by state.

Redistricting and Latent Competitiveness

The first stage of the empirical analysis is to examine the relationship between control of redistricting and the underlying latent competitiveness of U.S. House districts, as measured using the normalized presidential vote, following the approach of Abramowitz, Alexander, and Gunning (2006). Table 5.1 presents the results of several multivariate ordinary least squares (OLS) regression models exploring this relationship. Model 1 is the baseline model, including only the time trend and step functions for the two redistricting cycles during this period. Since the dependent variable seeks to capture the competitiveness of districts in the absence of confounding electoral effects, the inclusion of additional control variables is not necessary at this stage. Models 2 and 3 introduce the variables of primary interest, which are the measures of control of redistricting, including both the combined measure of partisan gerrymandering in model 2 and the separate dummy variables for Democratic and Republican gerrymandering in model 3. Perhaps the most interesting finding in table 5.1 is the negative and

TABLE 5.1. Redistricting and Latent Competitiveness in U.S. House Elections, 1990–2010

	(1)	(2)	(3)
Time Trend	−.124** (.035)	−.129** (.033)	−.136** (.034)
1990s Redistricting	.558 (.517)	.299 (.703)	.400 (.775)
2000s Redistricting	−.439 (.487)	−.450 (.489)	−.456 (.486)
Partisan Gerrymander	—	.647 (.549)	—
Democratic Gerrymander	—	—	.442 (.704)
Republican Gerrymander	—	—	.883 (.587)
Independent Commission	—	−.169 (.654)	−.155 (.652)
Judicial Redistricting	—	.404 (.600)	.338 (.628)
N	4,709	4,709	4,709

NOTES: Standard errors in parentheses. Models estimated using fixed-effects ordinary least squares (OLS) regression with robust standard errors clustered by state. $**p < .01$; $*p < .05$, two-tailed. Dependent variable is latent competitiveness. Unit of analysis is the House district. At-large states excluded.

statistically significant coefficient for the time trend variable. This indicates that U.S. House districts have been becoming, on average, less competitive over time at a rate of slightly more than .01 percent with each electoral cycle. Across the ten elections that make up the 1990s and 2000s redistricting cycles, the net effect of this trend is that the average House district in 2010 was approximately 1.2–1.4 percent less competitive than was the case in 1990. This is part of a long-term trend in which House districts have become progressively less competitive over time, and is highly consistent with the results of the analysis of Abramowitz, Alexander, and Gunning (2006) regarding the decline of competition in House elections.

Also consistent with their conclusions is the fact that none of the restricting variables reaches statistical significance in either model 2 or model 3, although each of the partisan gerrymandering effects is in the expected positive direction, and the effect of Republican gerrymandering only falls slightly short of significance at the .05 level. While this supports the notion that declining competition in House elections is not a by-product of redistricting, whether partisan, bipartisan, or conducted by a neutral party such as a commission or the courts, it also does not support the theoretical expectation that partisan gerrymandering would be associated with an increase in district-level competition. Nevertheless, the problems associated with using the normalized presidential vote as a measure of district competitiveness that were discussed earlier in this chapter would seem to caution against reading too much into these preliminary results. Of far greater interest and relevance to the theory of constrained redistricting is whether or not control of redistricting has any significant implications for the competitiveness of actual elections held during the subsequent decade.

Redistricting and Electoral Competitiveness

Table 5.2 presents the results of the OLS models of the competitiveness of U.S. House elections during the 1990s and 2000s redistricting cycles. Model 1 again is the baseline model, including the time trend, step functions for the 1990s and 2000s redistricting cycles, and the controls for the other determinants of electoral competitiveness. Model 2 also includes the combined partisan gerrymandering measure as well as variables to capture the effect of judicial redistricting and redistricting by an independent commission, while model 3 disaggregates the effects of partisan gerrymandering according to which party was in control of the redistricting process. Turning first to the baseline model 1, the step functions for each redistricting cycle demonstrate that while the 1990s redistricting had a negative and statistically significant effect on electoral competitiveness, most likely a result of the realignment occurring in the South, whereby marginal Democratic districts became increasingly Republican over the course of the decade, the 2000s cycle was not associated with any changes in district-level competitiveness. The coefficient for this variable, while negative, falls well short of statistical significance.

In keeping with previous research, the influence of money was also a significant predictor of district-level electoral competition (Abramowitz 1991; Abramowitz, Alexander, and Gunning 2006). The greater the discrepancy in campaign spending between the Democratic and Republican candidates in a district, the less competitive the election for that seat. Substantively, the effect of money on competitiveness is dramatic, with a 1-unit increase in the spending ratio, commensurate with moving from a situation of near spending parity to one where the vast majority of money in the district is spent by either the Democratic or Republican candidate, corresponding to a 20 percent decrease in competitiveness, or the equivalent of moving from a 50–50 tie to a 70–30 landslide. Surprisingly, once the influence of money is controlled for, the substantive

TABLE 5.2. Redistricting and Electoral Competitiveness in U.S. House Elections, 1990–2010

	(1)	(2)	(3)
Time Trend	.047 (.032)	.038 (.031)	.026 (.033)
1990s Redistricting	−1.532** (.516)	−2.380** (.492)	−2.191** (.490)
2000s Redistricting	−.318 (.312)	−.345 (.317)	−.357 (.308)
Partisan Gerrymander	—	1.347** (.326)	—
Democratic Gerrymander	—	—	.961* (.367)
Republican Gerrymander	—	—	1.791** (.404)
Independent Commission	—	1.389* (.678)	1.414* (.660)
Judicial Redistricting	—	1.263** (.337)	1.139** (.379)
Spending Ratio	−19.658** (.682)	−19.649** (.684)	−19.632** (.686)
Incumbency	−.568 (.382)	−.566 (.383)	−.579 (.382)
N	4,709	4,709	4,709

NOTES: Standard errors in parentheses. Models estimated using fixed-effects ordinary least squares (OLS) regression with robust standard errors clustered by state. **$p < .01$; *$p < .05$, two-tailed. Dependent variable is electoral competitiveness. Unit of analysis is the House district. At-large states excluded.

effects of incumbency are relatively modest. Not only is the coefficient for the presence of an incumbent in the race substantively small, associated with only a .5 percent reduction in electoral competitiveness, but it also falls short of statistical significance in each of the three models. This suggests, as previous research has demonstrated, that much of the electoral advantage enjoyed by incumbent House candidates seems to stem from their significant fund-raising advantages over challengers.

Models 2 and 3 introduce the variables designed to capture the effects of control of redistricting. The coefficients on each of the restricting variables therefore represent comparisons with the excluded category of bipartisan redistricting and provide the best test of the theoretical expectation that it is this variant that will prove most deleterious to electoral competition. Indeed, this is exactly what the results show. Model 2 includes a single variable for the effects of partisan gerrymandering rather than the measure disaggregated by party. It shows, as the theory predicted, that districts in states where redistricting was conducted through bipartisan compromise between Democrats and Republicans, the excluded category, were less competitive than those with any other type of redistricting, including partisan gerrymandering. Partisan redistricting states were associated with, on average, a 1.3 percent increase in district competitiveness as compared with bipartisan redistricting states, indicating that the results of U.S. House elections in those states were 1.3 percent closer to parity. Similar effects are observed for states in which redistricting was conducted by the courts, which were on average also approximately 1.3 percent more competitive than states with bipartisan redistricting, with both of these coefficients reaching statistical significance at the .01 level. Redistricting conducted by an independent commission was associated with an approximate 1.4 percent increase in electoral competitiveness over bipartisan redistricting, and this coefficient was significant at the .05 level.

Model 3, which includes separate measures of Democratic and Republican gerrymandering, reveals that the effects of Republican control of redistricting are indeed stronger than those of Democratic redistricting, increasing the competitiveness of House districts by almost 1.8 percent. This represents the largest substantive redistricting effect in any of the models. The effects of Democratic gerrymandering are also positive and statistically significant, corresponding to an almost 1 percent increase in district-level competitiveness. These results are consistent with the theory that bipartisan redistricting subverts electoral competition by creating safe districts for incumbents from both political parties, whereas partisan gerrymandering, in contrast, can create more competitive districts when redistricters pursue partisan advantage over incumbent protection.

A skeptical reader might nevertheless question the robustness of these findings, especially given that they challenge the conventional wisdom about the electoral consequences of partisan redistricting. While the models have attempted to control for other determinants of electoral competitiveness, it remains a possibility that there is some unobserved variable that is correlated with both control of redistricting and district-level competition, and that the relationship between partisan gerrymandering and competitiveness is thus a spurious one. Or it could be the case that there is some systematic relationship between states that have more competitive elections and states where partisan gerrymandering has taken place, thus explaining the positive relationship uncovered in the analysis. But to what extent is either of these possibilities a realistic one? While a spurious correlation between control of redistricting and competitiveness might arise within the context of a single redistricting cycle—it may just happen that the states where parties have unilateral control are coincidentally also the states that tend to have the most competitive House elections—it is extremely unlikely that such a situation would arise in two consecutive redistricting cycles. So the fact that the results are robust both across elections and redistricting cycles is cause to be confident that they are not spurious.

What about the likelihood of a systematic relationship between the competitiveness of elections in a state and control of redistricting introducing omitted variable bias into the models? In fact, there is more reason to expect the opposite to be true. Partisan redistricting requires that a party control both houses of the state legislature and the governorship, a situation that is actually less likely to occur in a highly competitive state and, conversely, more likely to happen in an uncompetitive state where a single political party is dominant. So if there is a systematic relationship between the competitiveness of elections in a state and control of redistricting, then we would expect it to work the other way, to bias the results against finding a positive relationship between partisan gerrymandering and competition. The fact that the positive effects of redistricting still emerge in the models is therefore cause for a great deal of confidence in the robustness of the results. Furthermore, the modeling strategy used by Friedman and Holden (2009), which is replicated here, serves to minimize the possibility of omitted variable bias by the inclusion of a time trend to capture the effects of any omitted variables that may be changing smoothly over time, and state fixed effects to account for differences between the states themselves, providing further confidence in the reliability of the results.

Overall then, the evidence from table 5.2 appears to be both robust and highly consistent. Partisan gerrymandering has a statistically significant and positive effect on the competitiveness of U.S. House elections, and during the two most recent redistricting cycles this effect is stronger for Republican gerrymandering than it is for Democratic gerrymandering. In combination with the bias results from chapter 4, this suggests that it is precisely where gerrymandering is the most effective that it also provides the biggest boost in competitiveness since the more efficient the gerrymander, the more seats the gerrymandering party must win by small electoral margins. The Republican Party's success during the 2000s redistricting cycle at leveraging its control of the redrawing of congressional district boundaries into subsequent electoral gains had the effect of creating more competitive elections in those states, providing strong support for the theory of constrained redistricting. The only question that remains to be answered, therefore, is to what extent this effect on district-level competitiveness translates into an increase in electoral responsiveness at the aggregate level. The first step toward investigating this is to examine the relationship between control of redistricting and seat change in subsequent elections.

Redistricting and Seat Change

The models in table 5.3 are a direct replication of those in table 5.2, with the only difference being the dependent variable. Here, the measure of electoral competitiveness is replaced with the measure of seat change discussed earlier, resulting in the estimation of a linear probability model where the coefficients represent the percentage change in the probability of a seat switching control from one party to the other in a given election. As is the case in chapter 4, estimating a logit or probit model produced no significant changes in the results or conclusions, and so the linear probability model is preferred for ease of interpretation.

Beginning with the baseline model 1, once again the time trend emerges as statistically significant, although this time in the positive direction, indicating that with each subsequent election after 1990 the probability of a given House

TABLE 5.3. Redistricting and Seat Change in U.S. House Elections, 1990–2010

	(1)	(2)	(3)
Time Trend	.005**	.005**	.004*
	(.001)	(.001)	(.002)
1990s Redistricting	−.027*	−.029	−.017
	(.013)	(.015)	(.016)
2000s Redistricting	−.039*	−.040*	.041*
	(.015)	(.015)	(.015)
Partisan Gerrymander	—	.008	—
		(.015)	
Democratic Gerrymander	—	—	−.016
			(.015)
Republican Gerrymander	—	—	.036*
			(.016)
Independent Commission	—	.039	.041
		(.022)	(.023)
Judicial Redistricting	—	−.005	−.012
		(.017)	(.015)
Spending Ratio	−.286**	−.286**	−.285**
	(.016)	(.016)	(.016)
Incumbency	−.132**	−.132**	−.132**
	(.021)	(.021)	(.021)
N	4709	4709	4709

NOTES: Standard errors in parentheses. Models estimated using fixed-effects ordinary least squares (OLS) regression with robust standard errors clustered by state. **$p < .01$; *$p < .05$, two-tailed. Dependent variable is the probability of a seat changing hands from one party to the other. Unit of analysis is the House district. At-large states excluded.

seat changing hands increased by 0.5 percent. Despite the decline in the average competitiveness of the underlying districts uncovered in table 5.1, these results suggest that by 2010, House seats were actually 5 percent more likely to change hands than they were in 1990. This may represent the combined effects of the rise of mid-decade redistricting and the extensive redistricting litigation that took place during the 1990s, which saw districts in numerous states being re-drawn more than once over the course of a single decade. This would likely have the effect of destabilizing district populations to a greater extent than would usually occur, making them more likely to shift partisan control from one election to the next.

Model 2 represents the baseline model with the additional inclusion of a variable to capture the effect of partisan gerrymandering overall, compared to bipartisan redistricting, as well as dummy variables for redistricting conducted by independent commissions and the courts. Unexpectedly, the effect of the combined partisan gerrymandering measure, while in the anticipated positive direction, falls short of statistical significance. One possible explanation for this is that, as occurred with the bias models in the previous chapter, combining both Democratic gerrymandering and Republican gerrymandering into a single variable is obscuring the statistically significant effects they may be having individually. This possibility is addressed in model 3, which includes separate variables for Democratic and Republican control of redistricting.

Turning to model 3, the results are remarkably consistent with the district-level analysis in chapter 4. Just as the effects of partisan redistricting on the probability of Democratic victory were largely confined to the Republican gerrymanders of the 2000s, so too the effects of gerrymandering on seat change only seemed to manifest themselves when the Republicans were in control of the process. The effect of Democratic gerrymandering on seat change in model 3 was close to zero and nowhere near statistical significance, while the effect of Republican gerrymandering was both positive and statistically significant. Overall, Republican gerrymanders were associated with an approximate 4 percent increase in the probability of districts switching control compared to states where redistricting was bipartisan. This is no doubt a relatively small effect, and only likely to be felt in the closest of House races, but nevertheless one that, when aggregated across all of the states where partisan gerrymandering occurs, is likely to produce a more responsive electoral environment.

Surprisingly, the effect of redistricting conducted by an independent commission, while positive, did not reach statistical significance, indicating that this method did not produce an overall increase in the probability of seat change compared to bipartisan redistricting. Similar results were uncovered for redistricting by the courts, where the coefficient was close to zero and also not statistically significant. This result may surprise many who criticize partisan redistricting for its detrimental effects on electoral competition and see commissions as the ideal solution to the problem of gerrymandering, as seats were no more likely to change hands in states where redistricting was conducted by an independent commission than they were in states where redistricting was bipartisan. The major finding in table 5.3, therefore, appears to be that, controlling for the other determinants of electoral competitiveness, seats in states with Republican-controlled partisan redistricting were significantly more likely to switch control from one party to the other than seats in states where there was no partisan redistricting, a result that runs directly counter to the conventional wisdom on the effects of gerrymandering.

Redistricting and Electoral Responsiveness

To what extent do the district-level effects uncovered in the previous sections translate into aggregate influences at the level of the state delegation or legislature as a whole? Figures 5.1 and 5.2 provide some evidence to suggest that partisan gerrymandering does indeed have a positive effect on overall electoral responsiveness. The graphs illustrate the level of responsiveness in House elections during the 1990s and 2000s redistricting cycles, disaggregated by the type of redistricting that occurred following the previous census. Electoral responsiveness was calculated using JudgeIt, and represents the expected change in a party's seat proportion given a 1 percent increase in its share of the popular vote. Larger values of electoral responsiveness indicate a greater seat change in the legislature in response to a shift in the vote share of 1 percent from one party to the other. A value of 2 on the responsiveness scale, therefore, corresponds to a situation where a 1 percent increase in the average vote share for Democratic candidates results in a 2 percent increase in the share of the overall seats won by Democratic candidates, while a value of 1 represents proportional representation—a 1 percent swing in the average vote produces a 1 percent shift in seats.

As the figures demonstrate, for both the 1990s (figure 5.1) and 2000s (figure 5.2) redistricting cycles, electoral responsiveness was consistently higher in states with partisan redistricting than it was in states with bipartisan redistricting, supporting the earlier district-level results based on the measure of electoral competitiveness. Though the levels of responsiveness for states with partisan versus bipartisan redistricting were only slightly higher throughout the 1990s, with the only significant difference being in 1994, responsiveness levels during the

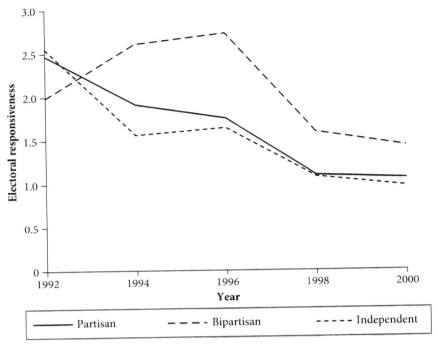

FIGURE 5.1. Control of Redistricting and Electoral Responsiveness, 1992–
2000

Note: Electoral responsiveness calculated using Judgelt II, v.1.4.1 (Gelman, King, and Thomas 2012).

2000s were substantially higher in partisan redistricting states, with the only exception being 2010. These results support the earlier conclusion that partisan redistricting leads to the creation of more competitive districts than bipartisan redistricting, and suggest that the truly deleterious effects on electoral responsiveness also seem to stem from bipartisan cooperation in redistricting rather than from partisan gerrymandering.

As a further robustness check, electoral responsiveness can also be estimated at the state level in a way similar to the bias analysis in chapter 4, and then included as the dependent variable in a multivariate regression model. Once again, however, the Judgelt estimation procedures limit this analysis to large states that provide sufficient observations for the quantities of interest to be estimated. Table 5.4 therefore represents a replication of table 4.6 in chapter 4, using responsiveness as the dependent variable instead of bias, and with a slightly different set of controls. The models omit the coattail variables and measure the popular vote using the margin of victory rather than Democratic vote share. Model 1 again represents the baseline model before any variables measuring control of redistricting

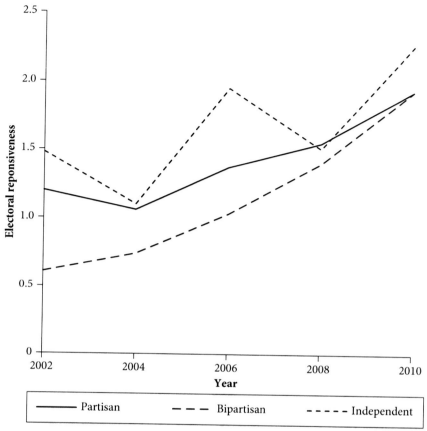

FIGURE 5.2. Control of Redistricting and Electoral Responsiveness, 2002–2010

Note: Electoral responsiveness calculated using Judgelt II, v.1.4.1 (Gelman, King, and Thomas 2012).

are included. Model 2 includes the combined measure of partisan gerrymandering in addition to the controls for independent and judicial redistricting, while model 3 contains both these controls and the measure of partisan gerrymandering disaggregated by party. The results are consistent with both the competitiveness analysis presented earlier and the aggregate measures of responsiveness illustrated in figures 5.1 and 5.2. Model 2 indicates that partisan control of the redistricting process is associated with a 0.5 percent increase in responsiveness, meaning that in those states, a 1 percent increase in vote share will produce a shift in seat proportion that is 0.5 percent greater than a corresponding increase in a state with bipartisan redistricting.

TABLE 5.4. Redistricting and Electoral Responsiveness in U.S. House Elections, 1990–2010

	(1)	(2)	(3)
Time Trend	−.029 (.020)	−.026 (.021)	−.027 (.022)
1990s Redistricting	.602+ (.312)	.295 (.347)	.304 (.349)
2000s Redistricting	−.139 (.213)	−.190 (.229)	−.204 (.229)
Partisan Gerrymander	—	.534* (.209)	—
Democratic Gerrymander	—	—	.479* (.217)
Republican Gerrymander	—	—	.568* (.263)
Independent Commission	—	−.119 (.241)	−.096 (.255)
Judicial Redistricting	—	.620* (.240)	.597* (.265)
Apportionment	−1.021* (.358)	−1.128** (.304)	−1.091* (.360)
Uncontested Districts	−.125* (.050)	−.132* (.055)	−.132* (.056)
Margin of Victory	1.948+ (.914)	1.846+ (1.029)	1.849 (1.038)
N	143	143	143

NOTES: Standard errors in parentheses. Models estimated using fixed-effects ordinary least squares (OLS) regression with robust standard errors clustered by state. **$p < .01$; *$p < .05$; +$p < .10$, two-tailed. Dependent variable is electoral responsiveness, calculated using Judgelt II, v.1.4.1 (Gelman, King, and Thomas 2012). Unit of analysis is the state house delegation. At-large states excluded.

As with the electoral competitiveness analysis in table 5.2, judicial redistricting is also associated with an increase in responsiveness, this time of 0.6 percent, while the independent commission variable is not only statistically insignificant but also in the negative direction, meaning that states in this category exhibited even lower levels of electoral responsiveness than those with bipartisan redistricting. These results are in keeping with the mixed conclusions drawn in the previous sections about the extent to which commissions do a good job of drawing competitive districts, where the effect of commissions on the district-level measures of electoral competition was inconsistent across different model specifications. Again consistent with the earlier analysis, when disaggregated by party, Republican gerrymandering was found to have a greater effect than Democratic gerrymandering, increasing responsiveness by 0.6 percent as opposed to

0.5 percent, with both showing a statistically significant difference over bipartisan redistricting.

As expected, the effects of redistricting on district-level competitiveness and seat change appear to translate into an aggregate effect on electoral responsiveness, and indicate that election results in states where partisan gerrymandering has occurred are more responsive to changes in voter preferences than in states where redistricting was bipartisan. This finding provides further support for the theoretical expectations regarding the effects of gerrymandering, and suggests a chain of causal relationships from redistricting to subsequent election results. Having control of the redrawing of district boundaries makes it more likely, although not guaranteed, that a party will attempt to increase its seat share in the legislature by manipulating those boundaries to produce an efficient gerrymander. When they are successful, the level of electoral bias and disproportionality within that state will increase, as the party will win more seats than its share of the popular vote would seem to predict.

However, the more efficient the gerrymander the more competitive districts must be drawn in order to maximize potential gains, and this has the unintended consequence of not only increasing the overall competitiveness of districts in the state, but the level of electoral responsiveness as well. The reason for this is that seats in states where effective partisan gerrymandering has occurred are more likely to switch hands in response to a subsequent shift in the popular vote than those in states where redistricting was bipartisan. Partisan gerrymandering, therefore, has the effect of increasing both bias and responsiveness, and these effects appear to go hand in hand with one another. The more effective the gerrymander is at biasing results in favor of the party in control of redistricting, the more responsiveness gets injected into the electoral system as a result, and the more likely it becomes that seats will change hands in response to changes in voter preferences in subsequent elections.

Conclusions

The results presented here support the theoretical expectation that bipartisan redistricting is more likely to protect incumbents due to collusion between the parties, whereas partisan redistricting is more likely to make incumbents of both parties vulnerable due to the emphasis on partisan advantage. Contrary to the conventional wisdom, partisan redistricting does not have damaging and detrimental effects for democracy in the form of diminished electoral competition. In fact, it contributes positively to the health of democracy by increasing electoral responsiveness in subsequent elections compared to its most frequent alternative, bipartisan redistricting.

Simply put, partisan redistricting allows the electoral system to better respond to the preferences of the public, as expressed by their votes in congressional elections, than it responds when redistricting has been conducted in a bipartisan manner. This indicates that recent efforts to try to outlaw partisan gerrymandering, either by challenging the practice in the federal courts in the hope that they will declare it unconstitutional or by transferring control of the redistricting process away from the political branches of government, may not be the panacea for democracy that many believe. In fact, in the two most recent redistricting cycles, redistricting conducted by independent commissions was statistically indistinguishable from bipartisan redistricting in terms of its implications for seat change, latent competitiveness, and electoral responsiveness, although it did have a positive effect on the electoral competitiveness of individual House districts.

These results have significant implications for the use of independent commissions to redraw district boundaries. Though they may make redistricting less prone to partisan influence, it is evident that commissions may not always have the positive democratic effects their proponents claim. Specifically, while the coefficient for redistricting by an independent commission was positive and significant in the district-level competitiveness analysis and positive but insignificant in the seat change analysis, it was actually negative in the responsiveness and latent competitiveness analyses, and in neither case did the variable reach statistical significance in any of the models. Further research is needed to ascertain more fully the effects of redistricting commissions, especially considering the small sample of states that utilized them during this period. However, the results presented here cast at least some doubt on whether taking the control of redistricting away from politicians is actually a healthy thing for democracy. Indeed, redistricting reformers would do well to focus more on the effects of redistricting than the intent of those who control the process.

Finally, the most significant takeaway from these results is that the biggest threat to democracy, in the form of the subversion of electoral competition, is not partisan gerrymandering but bipartisan redistricting. While the efficient gerrymander necessarily involves the creation of marginal districts, where redistricting is bipartisan, both parties have incentives to reduce competitiveness, resulting in redistricting plans that carve out safe districts for incumbents of both political stripes. Though critics of redistricting reform often focus on partisan gerrymandering and advocate the use of independent commissions as a solution to the negative effects of this practice, the empirical evidence supports neither of these conclusions. Conducting redistricting through an independent commission is no more beneficial for electoral competition than a partisan gerrymander, and may even be less so, while those who lament the decline in competition in U.S. House elections would do better to focus their energies on the influence of money and bipartisan collusion in redistricting than on the effects of gerrymandering. Redistricting reformers should focus their efforts on reducing the problems created by the practice of bipartisan redistricting rather than on the allegedly pernicious effects of partisan gerrymandering.

CONCLUSION

Implications for Redistricting Reform

These findings contradict much that has been written on the redistricting process in the United States, including the oft-repeated claims that partisan gerrymandering effectively dictates the results of subsequent elections and subverts electoral competition. They also undermine the significant criticism that has been directed toward the U.S. Supreme Court by many in the legal community for failing to thus far declare the practice unconstitutional. At the same time, they are very much in keeping with the existing consensus on partisan gerrymandering within the political science literature. Studies have repeatedly shown that redistricting is not responsible for either the decline in the competitiveness of House elections or the increase in partisan polarization, while the electoral effects of partisan gerrymandering have been shown to be variable but relatively modest. This chapter summarizes the major findings of the book and discusses their applicability to the present redistricting cycle that began following the 2010 Census. It also suggests some implications that these findings may have for redistricting policy and election law reform, and finally outlines some potential directions for profitable future research on this topic.

Redistricting in the 2010s

While the analysis in this book examines the implications of partisan control of the redistricting process for the results of congressional races in the 1990s and 2000s, it is the 2012 U.S. House election that has come to serve as the poster child for the damaging effects that can result when politicians are able to choose their own voters, rather than the voters being the ones to choose their politicians. Not only, it is alleged, has the American system of redistricting turned over to the foxes the responsibility for guarding the henhouse, but the feast has already begun. In 2012, the Democratic Party, having been consigned to minority status by its landslide defeat in the 2010 midterm election, won a total of almost 1.5 million more votes in House races across the nation than its Republican opponents, for a two-party popular vote total of 50.6 percent. Despite this, they won just 201 seats in the House to the Republicans' 234, adding just 8 to its 2010 total, while at the same time increasing its vote percentage by almost 5 percent. Not surprisingly, critics of partisan redistricting were quick to blame the gerrymander for Democrats' electoral woes.

Just as the 2000s cycle had seen the Republicans benefit from their control of state government in large states such as Texas, Pennsylvania, Florida, Michigan, Ohio, and Virginia, by virtue of their overwhelming victory in 2010, the Grand Old Party (GOP) again swept its way into power in state legislatures and governors' mansions across the country. According to the National Conference of State Legislatures (2011), prior to the 2010 election, the Democrats had enjoyed unified partisan control in sixteen states, twice as many as the Republicans' eight. The election in 2010, however, would completely flip the electoral landscape. By the time states began redrawing their district boundaries in 2011, there were just eleven states where the Democrats retained unified control of state government, while the Republicans had surged to twenty. These included fertile gerrymandering targets such as Florida, Georgia, Indiana, Michigan, Ohio, Texas, and Wisconsin. The results in chapter 4, however, which indicated that the Republicans' redistricting advantage following the 2000 election yielded them a surprising modest net seat advantage in House elections over the course of that decade, cast doubt on the likelihood of gerrymandering being responsible for all, or indeed most, of the pro-Republican bias in 2012.

This did not prevent the editorial pages of major newspapers from once again excoriating partisan gerrymandering for allowing self-interested politicians to effectively rig the results of subsequent elections. In the *New York Times,* Sam Wang (2013) decried "The Great Gerrymander of 2012," claiming that the Republican effort to take over state legislatures and use that control to influence redistricting was not only "highly successful," but amounted to a form of "partisan disenfranchisement." Dylan Matthews (2012) lamented in the *Washington Post* that "redistricting could keep the House red for a decade," highlighting the "truly bizarre district shapes" in some states where the GOP had redrawn the lines, and concluded that "it's going to be tough for Democrats to make big gains in the House until 2022, when the districts are drawn again following the Census." Finally, in the *Los Angeles Times*, David Horsey (2013) did not mince words in proclaiming that "short on voters, Republicans gerrymander their way back into power," even going as far as to state that "Republicans have become a devious party that believes if you cannot win by following fair rules, there is nothing wrong with rigging the game." Efforts by political scientists to counter this hyperbole—such as the *Washington Post* editorial by John Sides and Eric McGhee (2013), entitled "Redistricting Didn't Win Republicans the House"—were consistently drowned out by the negative coverage throughout the print media and blogosphere. Nevertheless, the point they make is well supported by the empirical evidence presented in this book: when confounding factors such as geography and incumbency are taken into account, the effects of gerrymandering all but vanish.

Policy Implications

These findings have a number of policy implications, in particular with regard to the redistricting reform movement and debates over the proper way to redraw electoral boundaries in a democratic system. To date, the major thrust in redistricting reform has been focused on efforts to remove control of the process from the political branches of government entirely, and instead create independent or bipartisan commissions to redraw the electoral boundaries after each census. These reforms have proceeded from the assumption that the major problem in the United States when it comes to redistricting is partisanship. Removing the partisan motivations of redistricters should, therefore, take care of what many see as the most pernicious element of the redistricting process: the manipulation of district boundaries to secure partisan gains. The results in this book suggest that this may not be the wisest strategy to pursue, and that the major problem in redistricting is not partisanship but incumbent protection. The focus of reforms should be based not on who controls redistricting, but on what their goals and incentives are. Far more so than partisanship, it is the extent to which those in control of the redistricting process seek to insulate their existing electoral strength that has the greatest implications for electoral competition and responsiveness.

Reformers should instead be focusing their efforts on how the process can be modified to prevent the subversive effects of incumbent protection gerrymanders. There are three possible mechanisms by which the redistricting process could be modified to place a greater emphasis on the creation of competitive districts. The first would follow a strategy similar to that of the existing redistricting reform movement, which has promoted the transfer of responsibility for redistricting to independent commissions, but with slight modifications. Previous reforms have generally created commissions that focus on the importance of following neutral principles in redistricting rather than overt partisanship. Yet, as the empirical analysis in this study demonstrates, these existing commissions have proven no more beneficial for electoral competition than partisan gerrymandering. Furthermore, some redistricting commissions are explicitly prohibited from considering political factors when redrawing district boundaries, a situation that may even decrease competitiveness by encouraging the creation of politically homogenous districts that follow the boundaries of existing political subdivisions.

In order to increase the competitiveness of House elections, redistricting commissions could be instructed to take the partisan affiliation of voters into account by giving them a legal mandate to create a certain percentage of competitive districts in the state. The advantage of this approach is that it works within the existing redistricting reform movement, while also preventing the redrawing of boundaries by political parties that many find so distasteful, thus making it more appealing politically. The disadvantage is that it must proceed on a state-by-state basis, either through the passage of legislation by state governments or, alternatively, by the people through ballot initiatives. It would also require the modification of the redistricting commissions that have already been created in a number of states in order to incorporate these additional guidelines.

A second approach would be to modify the constraints that redistricters already operate under to explicitly require them to consider district competitiveness as a criterion when redrawing congressional boundaries. Many states already require redistricters to take into account factors such as compactness, contiguity, and existing political, district, and community boundaries when crafting a redistricting plan. Florida's Amendment 6, passed through ballot initiative in the 2010 election, is an example how additional constraints on redistricters may be introduced, as it prohibits the drawing of districts "to favor or disfavor an incumbent or political party" (this language now appears in Article III, Section 20(a) of the Florida Constitution). A requirement that the competitiveness of districts also be taken into account would allow the redistricting process to increase competition without necessitating wholesale changes in how it operates in most states. The advantage of this approach is that it would prevent the most damaging incumbent protection gerrymanders from being implemented, without taking control of the redistricting process away from the political branches of government entirely. The disadvantage is that it also must proceed on a state-by-state basis, and since the involvement of incumbent politicians has been a source of much of the popular dissatisfaction with the current system, its political appeal may not be as great as alternatives, like Florida's Amendment 6, that focus explicitly on partisanship and incumbency.

The third approach stems directly from Article I, Section 4 of the Constitution, which, while reserving to the states the responsibility for determining the "times, places and manner of holding elections for Senators and Representatives," also gives Congress the power to "at any time by law make or alter such regulations." Several times in its history, Congress has used this power to place certain restrictions on the way states conduct congressional redistricting, including the present requirement that all members of the House be elected from single-member districts. It is within the powers of Congress to pass legislation mandating that states take the competitiveness of districts into account when redrawing congressional district boundaries, and even to require that states create a certain percentage of competitive districts within their jurisdictions. The advantage of this approach is that it could be achieved through a single law, passed by both houses of Congress and signed by the president, that would apply to the congressional redistricting process in every state. The disadvantage is that it would only apply to district boundaries for federal elections, as Congress has no power under Article I to dictate to the states how they must redraw their state legislative boundaries.

Whichever strategy is pursued, it is clear that the goals and approaches of the redistricting reform movement must be significantly reevaluated if redistricting reform is going to make a meaningful contribution to reversing the decline of competition in U.S. House elections and produce an electoral system that is more responsive to changes in voter preferences.

Future Directions

In this book, I examine the implications of control of redistricting for partisan bias, electoral disproportionality, competitiveness, and electoral responsiveness. However, these findings are based on an analysis of only the two most recent redistricting cycles, in the 1990s and 2000s. Future research should attempt to ascertain whether these conclusions hold for past redistricting cycles, in particular those in the 1970s and 1980s, where the involvement of the Supreme Court meant that for the first time all states were required to redraw their districts after every census. Of course, extending the analysis further back in time creates significant difficulties with regard to the collection of comparable data for past redistricting cycles, especially given that many of the primary sources relied on in this analysis are not available for previous decades. Nevertheless, an analysis of the consequences of redistricting for subsequent elections from a historical perspective would allow a much deeper understanding of the way the process operates under different contexts.

I also focus exclusively on U.S. House elections and the effects that redistricting in a state has on elections to that state's congressional delegation. Future research should therefore attempt to ascertain whether these findings are generalizable to state legislative elections, and whether dynamics underlie the electoral effects of redistricting in state elections that are similar to those in federal elections uncovered here. There is some reason to expect that there may be significant differences in the way that redistricting operates at the state legislative level. Most notably, those in control of the redistricting process are responsible for redrawing boundaries for entire legislative houses rather than just a single state's delegation. Thus, it is possible that state legislative redistricters are less constrained in their ability to use the process to secure partisan gains, potentially magnifying the effect of control of redistricting on partisan bias. An extension of this analysis to the state legislative level would also allow greater leverage for investigation of how the effects of redistricting vary according to structural and institutional factors. These could include the size of the legislative chamber, the use of multi-member districts, and the political heterogeneity of the state. The results of such an analysis would greatly inform policy debates on how best to ensure accountability and fairness in districting at all levels of government.

References

Abramowitz, Alan I. 1983. "Partisan Redistricting and the 1982 Congressional Elections." *Journal of Politics* 45: 767–70.

——. 1991. "Incumbency, Campaign Spending, and the Decline of Competition in U.S. House Elections." *Journal of Politics* 53: 34–56.

Abramowitz, Alan I., Brad Alexander, and Matthew Gunning. 2006. "Incumbency, Redistricting and the Decline of Competition in U.S. House Elections." *Journal of Politics* 68: 75–88.

Abramowitz, Alan I., and Kyle L. Saunders. 1998. "Ideological Realignment in the U.S. Electorate." *Journal of Politics* 60: 634–52.

American Political Science Association. 1950. "Toward a More Responsible Two-Party System: A Report of the Committee on Political Parties." *American Political Science Review* 44: part 2, supplement.

Ansolabehere, Stephen, and Alan Gerber. 1994. "The Mismeasure of Campaign Spending: Evidence from the 1990 U.S. House Elections." *Journal of Politics* 56: 1106–18.

Ansolabehere, Stephen, James M. Snyder Jr., and Charles Stewart III. 2000. "Old Voters, New Voters, and the Personal Vote: Using Redistricting to Measure Incumbency Advantage." *American Journal of Political Science* 44: 17–34.

Bishop, Bill. 2008. *The Big Sort: Why the Clustering of Like-Minded America Is Tearing Us Apart.* Boston: Houghton Mifflin Harcourt.

Black, Earl, and Merle Black. 2002. *The Rise of Southern Republicans.* Cambridge, MA: Harvard University Press.

Blais, André, and Agnieszka Dobrzynska. 1998. "Turnout in Electoral Democracies." *European Journal of Political Research* 33: 239–61.

Blumenthal, Ralph. 2003. "After Bitter Fight, Texas Senate Redraws Congressional Districts." *New York Times,* October 13, 2002.

Born, Richard. 1985. "Partisan Intentions and Election Day Realities in the Congressional Redistricting Process." *American Political Science Review* 79: 305–19.

——. 2000. "Congressional Incumbency and the Rise of Split-Ticket Voting." *Legislative Studies Quarterly* 25: 365–87.

Boston Globe. 2006. "Texas Massacre," July 29.

Bowler, Shaun, and Todd Donovan. 2011. "Electoral Competition and the Voter." *Public Opinion Quarterly* 75: 151–64.

Briffault, Richard. 2005. "Defining the Constitutional Question in Partisan Gerrymandering." *Cornell Journal of Law and Public Policy* 14: 397–421.

——. 2006. "*LULAC* on Partisan Gerrymandering: Some Clarity, More Uncertainty." *Michigan Law Review* 105: 58–62.

Brunell, Thomas L. 2008. *Redistricting and Representation: Why Competitive Elections Are Bad for America.* New York: Routledge.

Burnham, Walter Dean. 1974. "Communication." *American Political Science Review* 68: 207–13.

Butler, David, and Bruce Cain. 1992. *Congressional Redistricting: Comparative and Theoretical Perspectives.* New York: Macmillan.

Cain, Bruce. 1985. "Assessing the Partisan Effects of Redistricting." *American Political Science Review* 79: 320–33.

California Common Cause. 2006. *Survey Findings on Redistricting Reform in California.* Oakland, CA: California Common Cause.

Campagna, Janet, and Bernard Grofman. 1990. "Party Control and Partisan Bias in 1980s Congressional Redistricting." *Journal of Politics* 52: 1242–58.

Campbell, James E. 1986. "Presidential Coattails and Midterm Losses in State Legislative Elections." *American Political Science Review* 80: 45–63.

———. 1987. "The Revised Theory of Surge and Decline." *American Journal of Political Science* 31: 965–79.

———. 1996. *Cheap Seats: The Democratic Party's Advantage in U.S. House Elections.* Columbus: Ohio State University Press.

Campbell, James E., and Steve J. Jurek. 2003. "The Decline of Competition and Change in Congressional Elections." In *Congress Responds to the Twentieth Century,* edited by Sunil Ahuja and Robert Dewhirst. Columbus: Ohio State University Press.

Canon, David T. 2009. "Review of 'Redistricting and Representation: Why Competitive Elections Are Bad for America,' by Thomas Brunell." *Political Science Quarterly* 124: 366–68.

Capobianco, Neil A. 1988. "Political Gerrymandering: The Unconstitutional Threat to Fair Representation." *New York Law School Law Review* 33: 673–99.

Chapman, Steve. 2006. "The Court to Democracy: Drop Dead, Citizens." *Chicago Tribune,* July 2.

Cho, Wendy K. Tam, James G. Gimpel, and Iris S. Hui. 2013. "Voter Migration and the Geographic Sorting of the American Electorate." *Annals of the Association of American Geographers* 103 (4): 856–70. doi: 10.1080/00045608.2012.720229.

Congressional Quarterly. 1998. *Almanac of American Politics.* Washington, DC: CQ Press.

———. 2008. *Almanac of American Politics.* Washington, DC: CQ Press.

Cook, Charlie. 2005. "Mid-Decade Redistricting Grows More Popular." *Cook Political Report,* February 26. http://www.cookpolitical.com/node/2493 (accessed March 23, 2010).

Cox, Gary W., and Jonathan N. Katz. 2002. *Elbridge Gerry's Salamander: The Electoral Consequences of the Reapportionment Revolution.* New York: Cambridge University Press.

Crouch, Thomas H. 1987. "Political Gerrymandering: Judicial Scrutiny under the Equal Protection Clause." *Hamline Law Review* 10: 313–44.

Desposato, Scott W., and John R. Petrocik. 2003. "The Variable Incumbency Advantage: New Voters, Redistricting, and the Personal Vote." *American Journal of Political Science* 47: 18–32.

Dorf, Michael C. 2004. "The Supreme Court Gives Partisan Gerrymandering the Green Light—or at Least a Yellow Light." *FindLaw,* May 12. http://writ.news.findlaw.com /dorf/20040512.html (accessed December 12, 2007).

Eaton, Whitney M. 2006. "Where Do We Draw the Line? Partisan Gerrymandering in the State of Texas." *University of Richmond Law Review* 40: 1193–1228.

Economist. 2002. "How to Rig an Election." April 25.

Election Data Services. 2008. "2008 Reapportionment Analysis." *EDS,* December 22. http://www.electiondataservices.com/images/File/NR_Appor08wTables.pdf (accessed March 28, 2009).

Epstein, Lee. 2002. Foreword to *The U.S. Supreme Court and the Electoral Process,* 2nd ed., edited by David K. Ryden. Washington DC: Georgetown University Press.

Erikson, Robert S. 1972. "Malapportionment, Gerrymandering, and Party Fortunes in Congressional Elections." *American Political Science Review* 66: 1234–45.

Erikson, Robert S., and Thomas R. Palfrey. 1998. "Campaign Spending and Incumbency: An Alternative Simultaneous Equations Approach." *Journal of Politics* 60: 355–73.

Evans, Heather K. 2013. "The Lasting Effect of Competitive Elections on Congressional Approval: Evidence from the 2010 and 2011 Cooperative Congressional Election Study." *Electoral Studies* 32: 779–82.

Evans, Heather K., Michael J. Ensley, and Edward G. Carmines. 2014. "The Enduring Effects of Competitive Elections." *Journal of Elections, Public Opinion and Parties* 24: 455–72.

Fenno, Richard F. 1978. *Home Style: House Members in Their Districts.* Boston: Little, Brown.

Ferejohn, John A. 1977. "On the Decline of Competition in Congressional Elections." *American Political Science Review* 71: 16, 76.

Flavin, Patrick, and Gregory Shufeldt. 2015. "State Party Competition and Citizens' Political Engagement." *Journal of Elections, Public Opinion, and Parties* 25: 444–62.

Franklin, Mark N. 2004. *Voter Turnout and the Dynamics of Electoral Competition in Established Democracies since 1945.* New York: Cambridge University Press.

Friedman, John, and Richard T. Holden. 2008. "Optimal Gerrymandering: Sometimes Pack but Never Crack." *American Economic Review* 98: 113–34.

——. 2009. "The Rising Incumbency Advantage: What's Gerrymandering Got to Do with It?" *Journal of Politics* 71: 593–611.

Geldzahler, Evan. 1988. "*Davis v. Bandemer:* Remedial Difficulties in Political Gerrymandering." *Emory Law Journal* 37: 443–93.

Gelman, Andrew, and Gary King. 1994. "Enhancing Democracy through Legislative Redistricting." *American Political Science Review* 88: 541–59.

Gelman, Andrew, Gary King, and Andrew C. Thomas. 2012. *JudgeIt II: A Program for Evaluating Electoral Systems and Redistricting Plans.* Version 1.4.1. http://gking .harvard.edu/judgeit (accessed May 25, 2013).

Gierzynski, Anthony, and David Breaux. 1993. "Money and the Party Vote in State House Elections." *Legislative Studies Quarterly* 18: 515–33.

Gilligan, Thomas W., and John G. Matsusaka. 1999. "Structural Constraints on Partisan Bias under the Efficient Gerrymander." *Public Choice* 100: 65–84.

Gimpel, James G., and Jason E. Schuknecht. 2003. *Patchwork Nation: Sectionalism and Political Change in American Politics.* Ann Arbor: University of Michigan Press.

Glazer, Amihai, Bernard Grofman, and Marc Robbins. 1987. "Partisan and Incumbency Effects in the 1970s Congressional Redistricting." *American Journal of Political Science* 30: 680–701.

Gopoian, J. David, and Darrell M. West. 1984. "Trading Security for Seats: Strategic Considerations in the Redistricting Process." *Journal of Politics* 46: 1080–96.

Greene, Jamal. 2005. "Judging Partisan Gerrymanders under the Elections Clause." *Yale Law Review* 114: 1021–61.

Griffith, Elmer C. 1974. *The Rise and Development of the Gerrymander.* New York: Arno Press.

Grofman, Bernard. 1982. "Alternatives to Single-Member Plurality Districts: Legal and Empirical Issues." *Policy Studies Journal* 9: 875–98.

——. 1983. "Measures of Bias and Proportionality in Seats-Votes Relationships." *Political Methodology* 9: 295–327.

——. 1990. "Unresolved Issues in Partisan Gerrymandering Litigation." In *Political Gerrymandering and the Courts,* edited by Bernard Grofman. New York: Agathon.

Grofman, Bernard, and Thomas L. Brunell. 2005. "The Art of the Dummymander: The Impact of Recent Redistrictings on the Partisan Makeup of Southern House Seats." In *Redistricting in the New Millennium,* edited by Peter F. Galderisi. New York: Lexington Books.

Grofman, Bernard, and Gary King. 2007. "The Future of Partisan Symmetry as a Judicial Test for Partisan Gerrymandering after *LULAC v. Perry." Election Law Journal* 6: 2–35.

Hefley, Joel, and Alan B. Mollohan. 2004. "Letter to the Honorable Tom DeLay." Washington, DC: U.S. House of Representatives Committee on Standards of Official Conduct, October 6. http://www.house.gov/ethics/DeLay_letter.htm (accessed November 23, 2007).

Hibbing, John R., and Elizabeth Theiss-Morse. 1995. *Congress as Public Enemy: Public Attitudes toward American Political Institutions.* New York: Cambridge University Press.

———. 2002. *Stealth Democracy: Americans' Beliefs about How Government Should Work.* New York: Cambridge University Press.

Hirsch, Sam. 2003. "The United States House of Representatives: What Went Wrong with the Latest Round of Congressional Redistricting." *Election Law Journal* 2: 179–216.

Hofstadter, Richard. 1970. *The Idea of a Party System: The Rise of Legitimate Opposition in the United States, 1740–1840.* Berkeley: University of California Press.

Horsey, David. 2013. "Short of Voters, Republicans Gerrymander Their Way Back into Power." *Los Angeles Times*, February 6.

Issacharoff, Samuel, and Pamela S. Karlan. 2004. "Where to Draw the Line? Judicial Review of Political Gerrymanders." *University of Pennsylvania Law Review* 153: 541–78.

Jacobson, Gary C. 1990. *The Electoral Origins of Divided Government: Competition in U.S. House Elections, 1946–1988.* Boulder, CO: Westview.

———. 1993. "Getting the Details Right: A Comment on 'Changing Meanings' of Electoral Marginality in U.S. House Elections, 1824–1978." *Political Research Quarterly* 46: 49–54.

Jewell, Malcolm E., and Sarah M. Morehouse. 2001. *Political Parties and Elections in American States*, 4th ed. Washington, DC: CQ Press.

Jewett, Aubrey. 2013. "'Fair' Districts in Florida: New Congressional Seats, New Constitutional Standards, Same Old Republican Advantage?" In *The Political Battle over Congressional Redistricting at the State Level*, edited by William Miller and Jeremy Walling. Lanham, MD: Lexington Books.

Jones, Philip Edward. 2013. "The Effect of Political Competition on Democratic Accountability." *Political Behavior* 35: 481–515.

Kang, Michael S. 2005. "The Bright Side of Partisan Gerrymandering." *Cornell Journal of Law and Public Policy* 14: 443–70.

Karch, Andrew, Corrine M. McConnaughy, and Sean M. Theriault. 2007. "The Legislative Politics of Congressional Redistricting Commission Proposals." *American Politics Research* 35: 808–25.

Kastellec, Jonathan P., Andrew Gelman, and Jamie Chandler. 2008. "Predicting and Dissecting the Seats-Votes Curve in the 2006 U.S. House Election." *PS: Political Science and Politics* 41: 139–45.

Katz, Ellen D. 2007. "Reviving the Right to Vote." *Ohio State Law Journal* 68: 1163–82.

Keith, Bruce E., David B. Magleby, Candice J. Nelson, Elizabeth Orr, and Mark C. Westlye. 1992. *The Myth of the Independent Voter.* Berkeley: University of California Press.

Kenny, Christopher, and Michael McBurnett. 1994. "An Individual-Level Multiequation Model of Expenditure Effects in Contested House Elections." *American Political Science Review* 88: 699–707.

Key, V. O. 1955. *Southern Politics in State and Nation.* Knoxville: University of Tennessee Press.

———. 1956. *American State Politics: An Introduction.* New York: Knopf.

King, Gary. 1989. "Representation through Legislative Redistricting: A Stochastic Model." *American Journal of Political Science* 33: 787–824.

King, Gary, and Robert X. Browning. 1987. "Democratic Representation and Partisan Bias in Congressional Elections." *American Political Science Review* 81: 1251–73.

King, Gary, and Andrew Gelman. 1991. "Systematic Consequences of Incumbency Advantage in U.S. House Elections." *American Journal of Political Science* 35: 110–38.

King, Gary, Bernard Grofman, Andrew Gelman, and Jonathan Katz. 2005. "Amicus Brief in *Jackson v. Perry*, Submitted on Behalf of Neither Party." *U.S. Supreme Court* (No. 05-276).

La Raja, Raymond. 2009. "Redistricting: Reading between the Lines." *Annual Review of Political Science* 12: 203–23.

Lazarus, Edward. 2003. "The Supreme Court Considers Sophisticated Political Gerrymandering: Are Voting Rights Preserved if Boundaries Are Drawn to Ensure Particular Election Outcomes?" *FindLaw*, December 25. http://writ.lp.findlaw.com /lazarus/20031225.html (accessed December 12, 2007).

———. 2005. "Why Judge Alito's View on 'One Person, One Vote' May Be Even More Important than His View on Roe v. Wade." *FindLaw*, December 9. http://writ.news .findlaw.com/lazarus/20051209.html (accessed 2/23/07).

Leavenworth, Stuart. 2010. "Gerrymandering Hurts Cities Such as Elk Grove." *Sacramento Bee*, February 21.

Lipsitz, Keena. 2011. *Competitive Elections and the American Voter*. Philadelphia: University of Pennsylvania Press.

Lowenstein, Daniel H. 2005. "*Vieth*'s Gap: Has the Supreme Court Gone from Bad to Worse on Partisan Gerrymandering?" *Cornell Journal of Law and Public Policy* 14: 367–95.

Lublin, David, and Michael P. McDonald. 2006. Is It Time to Draw the Line? The Impact of Redistricting on Competition in State House Elections." *Election Law Journal* 5: 144–57.

Macedo, Stephen. 2009. *Democracy at Risk: How Political Choices Undermine Citizen Participation, and What We Can Do about It*. Washington, DC: Brookings University Press.

Madison, James. 1787. "Federalist No. 10." *The Federalist Papers*. New York: J. and A. McLean.

Matthews, Dylan. 2012. "How Redistricting Could Keep the House Red for a Decade." *Washington Post*, November 8.

Mayhew, David R. 1971. "Congressional Representation: Theory and Practice in Drawing the Districts." In *Reapportionment in the 1970s*, edited by Nelson W. Polsby. Berkeley: University of California Press.

McDonald, Ian. 2011. "Migration and Sorting in the American Electorate: Evidence from the 2006 Cooperative Congressional Election Study." *American Politics Research* 39: 512–533.

McDonald, Michael P. 2006. "Drawing the Line on District Competition." *PS: Political Science and Politics* 39: 91–94.

McKee, Seth C. 2008. "The Effects of Redistricting on Voting Behavior in Incumbent U.S. House Elections, 1992–1994." *Political Research Quarterly* 61: 122–33.

McKee, Seth C., Jeremy M. Teigen, and Mathieu Turgeon. 2006. "The Partisan Impact of Congressional Redistricting: The Case of Texas, 2001–2003." *Social Science Quarterly* 87: 308–17.

Mills, Karen M. 2001. "Congressional Apportionment: Census 2000 Brief." U.S. Census Bureau. https://www.census.gov/prod/2001pubs/c2kbr01-7.pdf (accessed November 23, 2015).

Mixon, Franklin G., and Kamal P. Upadhyaya. 1997. "Gerrymandering and the Voting Rights Act of 1982: A Public Choice Analysis of Turnover in the U.S. House of Representatives." *Public Choice* 93: 357–71.

Monmonier, Mark. 2001. *Bushmanders and Bullwinkles: How Politicians Manipulate Electronic Maps and Census Data to Win Elections.* Chicago: University of Chicago Press.

National Conference of State Legislatures. 2008. *Outline of Redistricting Litigation in the 1990s.* http://www.senate.mn/departments/scr/redist/redout.htm (accessed December 13, 2007).

——. 2011. *2011 State and Legislative Partisan Composition.* http://www.ncsl.org/documents/statevote/2010_Legis_and_State_post.pdf (accessed March 5, 2016).

New York Times. 2005. "Redistricting Tom DeLay." December 14.

——. 2006. "The Texas Gerrymander." March 1.

Niemi, Richard G., and John Deegan Jr. 1978. "A Theory of Political Districting." *American Political Science Review* 72: 1304–23.

Niemi, Richard G., and Laura R. Winsky. 1992. "The Persistence of Partisan Redistricting Effects in Congressional Elections, in the 1970s and 1980s." *Journal of Politics* 54: 565–72.

Niemi, Richard G., and Stephen Wright. 1990. "Majority-Win Percentages: An Approach to the Votes-Seats Relationship in Light of *Davis v. Bandemer.*" In *Political Gerrymandering and the Courts,* edited by Bernard Grofman. New York: Agathon.

Note. 2004. "A New Map: Partisan Gerrymandering as a Federalism Injury." *Harvard Law Review* 117: 1196–1214.

O'Brien, David M. 2005. *Constitutional Law and Politics: Volume One—Struggles for Power and Governmental Accountability.* New York: W. W. Norton.

Owen, Guillermo, and Bernard Grofman. 1988. "Optimal Partisan Gerrymandering." *Political Geography Quarterly* 7: 5–22.

Petrocik, John R., and Scott W. Desposato. 1998. "The Partisan Consequences of Majority-Minority Redistricting in the South, 1992 and 1994." *Journal of Politics* 60: 613–33.

Pew Research Center. 2006. "Lack of Competition in Elections Fails to Stir Public." Pew Research Center, October 27.

Public Policy Institute of California. 2007. *Californians and Their Government.* San Francisco: Public Policy Institute of California.

Ranney, Austin. 1965. "Parties in State Politics." In *Politics in the American States: A Comparative Analysis,* edited by Herbert Jacob and Kenneth N. Vines. Boston: Little, Brown.

——. 1975. *Curing the Mischiefs of Faction: Party Reform in America.* Berkeley: University of California Press.

Ratcliffe, R. G., Polly Ross Hughes, and Amy Raskin. 2003. "Wanted: AWOL Democrats; Some Rebel Lawmakers Surface in Oklahoma." *Houston Chronicle,* May 13.

Ratliff, John. 2003. "Texas Republicans Crossed the Line This Time." *Washington Post,* October 19.

Rives, William C. 1970. *History of the Life and Times of James Madison.* Boston: Little, Brown.

Rogerson, Peter, and Z. Yang. 1999. "The Effects of Spatial Population Distributions and Political Districting on Minority Representation." *Social Science Computer Review* 17: 27–39.

Rosenbaum, David E. 2004. "Justices Bow to Legislators in Political Gerrymandering Case." *New York Times,* April 29.

Schattschneider, E. E. 1942. *Party Government.* New York: Holt, Rinehart and Winston.

Seabrook, Nicholas R. 2010. "Money and State Legislative Elections: The Conditional Impact of Political Context." *American Politics Research* 38: 399–424.

Shotts, Kenneth W. 2001. "The Effect of Majority-Minority Mandates on Partisan Gerrymandering." *American Journal of Political Science* 45: 120–35.

Sides, John, and Eric McGhee. 2013. "Redistricting Didn't Win Republicans the House." *Washington Post*, February 17.

St. Louis Post Dispatch. 2006. "Democracy's Bad Week." July 2.

Toobin, Jeffrey. 2006. "Drawing the Line: Will Tom Delay's Redistricting in Texas Cost Him His Seat?" *New Yorker,* March 6.

Tufte, E. R. 1973. "The Relationship between Seats and Votes in Two-Party Systems." *American Political Science Review* 67: 540–54.

Voting and Democracy Research Center. 2004. *Mapping Our Future: A Public Interest Guide to Redistricting 2000.* http://archive.fairvote.org/index.php?page=289 (accessed December 13, 2007).

Wang, Sam. 2013. "The Great Gerrymander of 2012." *New York Times*, February 2.

Washington Post. 2005. "Redistricting Reconsidered: Does Election 2006 Show that Fears about Partisan Gerrymandering Were Overblown?" November 15.

——. 2006. "Drawing Lines on Lines." March 8.

Yoshinaka, Antoine, and Chad Murphy. 2011. "The Paradox of Redistricting: How Partisan Mapmakers Foster Competition but Disrupt Representation." *Political Research Quarterly* 64: 435–77.

Zaller, John. 1994. *Securing the District.* NES Pilot Study Report, No. nes008227.

Court Cases

Anne Arundel County Republican Central Comm. v. State Administrative Bd. of Election Laws, 781 F. Supp. 394 (Md. 1991), summarily aff'd, 504 U.S. 938 (1992)
Badham v. Eu, 694 F. Supp. 664 (N.D. Cal. 1988), summarily aff'd, 488 U.S. 1024 (1989)
Baker v. Carr, 369 U.S. 186 (1962)
Board of Estimate of City of New York v. Morris, 489 U.S. 688 (1989)
Buckley v. Valeo, 424 U.S. 1 (1976)
Bush v. Gore, 531 U.S. 98 (2000)
Bush v. Vera, 517 U.S. 952 (1996)
California Democratic Party v. Jones, 530 U.S. 567 (2000)
Citizens United v. FEC, 558 U.S. 310 (2010)
Colegrove v. Green, 328 U.S. 549 (1946)
Colorado General Assembly v. Salazar, 124 S. Ct. 2228 (2004)
Colorado Republican Federal Campaign Committee v. FEC, 518 U.S. (1996)
Cook v. Gralike, 531 U.S. 510 (2001)
Cox v. Larios, 300 F. Supp. 1320 (N.D. Ga. 2004), summarily aff'd, 542 U.S. 947 (2004)
Davis v. Bandemer, 478 U.S. 190 (1986)
Fund for Accurate and Informed Representation, Inc. v. Weprin, 796 F. Supp. 662 (N.D. NY), summarily aff'd, 506 U.S. 1017 (1992)
Georgia v. Ashcroft, 539 U.S. 461 (2003)
Holder v. Hall, 512 U.S. 874 (1995)
Holloway v. Hechler, 817 F. Supp. 617 (S.D. W. Va. 1992), summarily aff'd, 507 U.S. 956 (1993)
Hunt v. Cromartie, 526 U.S. 541 (1999)
Hunt v. Cromartie, 532 U.S. 234 (2001)
Jacobellis v. Ohio, 378 U.S. 184 (1964)
Johnson v. De Grandy, 512 U.S. 997 (1994)
Karcher v. Daggett, 462 U.S. 725 (1983)
Kirkpatrick v. Preisler, 394 U.S. 526 (1969)
Larios v. Cox, 124 S. Ct. 2806 (2004)
Lawyer v. Department of Justice, 521 U.S. 567 (1997)
League of United Latin American Citizens v. Perry, 548 U.S. 399 (2006)
McConnell v. FEC, 540 U.S. 93 (2003)
Meadows v. Moon, 521 U.S. 1113 (1997)
Miller v. Johnson, 515 U.S. 900 (1995)
Mobile v. Bolden, 446 U.S. 55 (1980)
Northwest Austin Municipal Utility District v. Holder, 557 U.S. 193 (2009)
O'Lear v. Miller, 222 F. Supp. 2d 850 (E.D. Mich.), summarily aff'd, 537 U.S. 997 (2002)
Pope v. Blue, 809 F. Supp. 392 (W.D. N.C. 1992), summarily aff'd, 506 U.S. 801 (1992)
Republican Party of North Carolina v. Hunt, 77 F.3d 470 (1996)

Republican Party of North Carolina v. Martin, 980 F.2d 943 (1992)
Reynolds v. Sims, 377 U.S. 533 (1964)
Salazar v. Davidson, 79 P.3d 1221 (Colo. 2003)
San Antonio Independent School District v. Rodriguez, 411 U.S. 1 (1973)
Shaw v. Hunt, 517 U.S. 899 (1996)
Shaw v. Reno, 509 U.S. 630 (1993)
Shelby County v. Holder, 570 U.S. (2013)
Thornburg v. Gingles, 478 U.S. 30 (1986)
U.S. Term Limits Inc. v. Thornton, 514 U.S. 779 (1995)
Vieth v. Jubelirer, 541 U.S. 267 (2004)
Vieth v. Pennsylvania, 195 F. Supp. 2d 672 (M.D. Pa. 2002)
Wesberry v. Sanders, 376 U.S. 1 (1964)
Whitcomb v. Chavis, 403 U.S. 124 (1971)
Wilkins v. West, 571 S.E. 2d 100 (Va. 2002)

Index